CW00351016

CHOOSING A
NAME FOR
YOUR BABY

HAMLYN HELP YOURSELF GUIDE

CHOOSING A NAME FOR YOUR BABY

Edited by
SUZY POWLING

HAMLYN

First Published in 1989 by
The Hamlyn Publishing Group Limited
a division of the Octopus Publishing Group
Michelin House
81 Fulham Road London
SW3 6RB

© The Hamlyn Publishing Group Limited 1989

ISBN 0 600 56638 2

Printed and bound in Great Britain by
The Guernsey Press Co. Ltd., Guernsey, Channel Islands.

CONTENTS

INTRODUCTION

Choosing a name for your baby is an exciting and important decision. Every name has its own associations, meanings and abbreviations and if both you and your child are to be happy with your choice, you will want to take them all into account.

This book gives full details of over 700 boys' and girls' names, some popular and long-established, others unusual, to help you make the right decision. You can turn to any name to check on the usual range of pet forms because, even if you avoid them, they will probably be used by friends and relatives. You may find that there is an attractive alternative form or spelling which will tempt you to choose a particular name. Whether or not you think the original meaning of a name important, you will want to make sure that it has no unpleasant or unfortunate associations.

When you begin to look at various names you will find that many factors will affect your particular choice. You may decide on a name because it has personal associations; perhaps it brings back memories of someone you love or of a special event. More likely, it is because the name creates the right image in your mind.

The first associations of any name come from its meaning and our ancestors thought that names had magical powers, so that their meanings could affect the child's future. Nowadays, when many meanings are forgotten or overlooked for the sake of a pleasant sound, there are still happy names like Daryl (beloved), Hilary (cheerful), Alma (kind), Karenza (love) and Isaac (laughter), virtuous names like Faith, Honor, Patience and Constance and strong prosperous names like Donald (world-ruler), Damian (one who tames), Gary (spear-brave), Audrey (noble strength) and Bernice (bringer of victory).

Quite apart from their direct meaning, names have their own special 'feel', so that we immediately form some sort of mental picture of the person behind the name and it can be quite a jolt if we

7

find that the person is quite different from that first picture. Consider what kind of personality you will be encouraging in your child. If Gladys grows up to be impetuous and trendy or Melanie is brusque and bad tempered, it may take new friends a while to adjust to a character so unlike the image associated with the name. To most of us a dignified Victoria, friendly Robert or hearty Monica seem aptly named; not many of us would think that a sporty outdoor Giselle, a studious, retiring Clint or a beefy, weightlifting Cyril had names that suited their personalities.

The sound of the name is also important. You will need to test whether it blends well with your surname, whether it flows easily or makes an awkward tongue twister. A one-syllable surname may sound better when balanced by a longer first name and you may want to enhance a common surname with an uncommon first name but remember that children do not always thank their parents for a name which is so unusual that it always causes comment. If you have a surname which has an obvious meaning of its own, like Bush or Tree, then Rose or Holly might not be the happiest choice.

A second personal name can be useful in future years, if for some reason your child dislikes his or her first name, but always remember to check that the resulting initials do not make an unpleasant joke of their own. A child whose initials are S.A.P. or W.E.T. will have a ready-made and unwelcome nickname!

Though few of us go to the trouble of adopting a new name, a pet name can often do the trick. Reginald has an upright, responsible ring to it but Rex sounds far more dashing. Teddy sounds more easy-going than Edward, Al sounds more of a tomboy than Alison and Meg sounds more homely than Margaret.

Some names are distinctly more aristocratic-sounding than others, usually those with several syllables and a long history like Nicholas, Benedict, Julian, Isabel, Alexandra or Cassandra. However, rather than using established names you may like the idea of deciding on a name which is riding high in current fashion but it is wise to consider whether or not it will wear well. Some names seem to survive through every generation, others are favourites in one decade and fall out of use in the next.

For instance, after the Restoration the 17th century Puritans thumbed through the Bible to find sober, respectable names like Abel, Caleb and Gideon or gave their children names with a high moral tone like Hope, Mercy and Prudence.

In the 18th century, pet forms of girls' names began to come into their own with Betty, Nancy, Peggy and Molly used independently, instead of being only diminutives of Elizabeth, Ann, Margaret and Mary.

The Victorians had a great affection for names taken from nature, particularly pretty flower names, so many girls were called Ivy, Violet, Iris, Primrose, Myrtle, and Lily. Rosemary, Laurel, Heather and Hazel all emerged at the same time but have lasted well since. A little later came jewel names like Amber and Coral which are still popular today.

The elaborate boys' names beloved of the Victorians – Percival, Clarence, Cuthbert, Herbert, Horace – have gone out of use, replaced by a modern fashion for short, no-nonsense names like Drew, Dean or Gary. Many of the female names of Victorian times like Bertha and Gertrude have disappeared but others, like Charlotte, Emily and Hannah, are back in favour.

Short, brisk names like Dee, Kay, Jake or Drew make an active no-nonsense impression. Today's romance writers choose pseudonyms like Juliet, Miranda, Rebecca or Suzanne to give themselves the right image, while they give their heroes names which are instantly identifiable as 'manly': Bruce, Blair, Craig or Grant.

There are countless other influences and events that have provided a wealth of names over the years – whether they have added to the esteem of an existing name, revived one lost over the years or given rise to something completely new. Here are a selection of some of the most popular . . .

Royal Names

The Prince and Princess of Wales followed a long tradition by naming their second baby Henry and announcing that he would be called Harry. England's eight King Henrys were all known as Harry, which was the nearest the English could come to giving the name its original French pronunciation 'Henri'. Their choice will probably mean that Henry, which had almost slipped out of use, will come right back into fashion again, just as William did after their elder son's birth in 1982. The Duke and Duchess of York also followed suit when they named their first child 'Beatrice', this created a sensation in 1988 as the name had not been popular since Victorian times.

Tradition always plays a vital part in the naming of royal babies, especially those nearest in succession to the throne. William has a noble pedigree dating from the reign of William the Conqueror when, in honour of a powerful monarch, it became the most popular name in the country and remained as top favourite for 200 years. For their eldest son, the Queen and Prince Philip revived a name which had not been used in the family since the end of the Stuart dynasty. James Stuart named his son Charles, after the many successful monarchs who had borne the name, hoping that it would bring luck to his unfortunate family. Though the luck never materialized, the name stayed in use.

If Queen Victoria had had her way, our future king would have been called after her beloved husband. It was her plan that her eldest son, Albert Edward, would become Albert I and be succeeded by a long line of Alberts, but her son chose to become Edward VII.

It was Victoria herself who began a royal habit of discarding her first name. She was christened Alexandrina after her godfather Tsar Alexander of Russia but she insisted on dropping it once she became queen. The name Victoria was almost unknown here at the time and was an English version of her German mother's name Victoire. Several other girls' names arrived in Britain along with foreign princesses such as Eleanor of Aquitaine, wife of Henry II, Adelaide of Saxe-Coburg Meiningen, who married William IV and Caroline of Anspach, wife of George II.

Royal babies usually have a string of middle names, in honour of godparents, aunts, uncles and ancestors, so parents who want a less obvious 'royal' name for their own baby have a wide choice. Queen Mary, wife of George V, holds the royal record for baptismal names – Victoria Mary Augusta Louisa Olga Pauline Claudia Agnes – and some of the more surprising middle names of the present family include Christian (Prince Andrew), Franklin (Prince Michael), Christabel (Princess Alexandra) and Ophelia (Lady Gabriella 'Ella' Windsor).

Place Names

A surprising number of personal names have their roots in place names, which turned into surnames in the Middle Ages, when one of the simplest ways of distinguishing one man from another was to call him by the name of the village or area where he lived. Centuries later parents who were searching for ideas used surnames as given names, especially for boys, just because they liked the sound of them.

Some of the descriptive place names which have found their way into the birth register are Douglas (dark water), Leslie (little meadow), Denton (farm in the valley), Clifford (ford near a slope), Clifton (settlement near a slope), Bradley (broad clearing), Kingsley (king's wood), Blair (flat land) and Carlton (peasant's farm).

In the 19th century there was a vogue for aristocratic sounding first names and parents began borrowing the surnames of leading families of the time, among them Wyndham (Wyman's settlement), Warwick (dwelling near a wier) and Dudley (Duda's clearing). As many of the noble families of England had Norman ancestors, French place names often crop up. Montague derives from Mont Aigue near Caen, Vernon from Vernon in Eure, Courtenay from Courtenay in the Ile de France and, from towns in Normandy, come Percy from Perci, Neville from Neuville and Bruce from Brieuse.

Nola and Roma come straight from the names of Italian towns and Florence only became popular in the 19th century through the fame of pioneering nurse Florence Nightingale, who was christened after her Italian birthplace. Another group of names with their roots firmly among the ancient Greeks or Romans were originally given to immigrants from other towns, regions or countries to mark them out from the local residents, so that Adrian was the name for 'a man from Adria', Doris for 'a woman of Doris', Dacian was a native of Dacia, Luke came from Lucania and Alban from Alba.

Parents have been more wary of adopting family names for baby girls. Shelley, which means 'clearing on a slope' and Shirley, which means 'shire meadow' both began as boys' names and only later came into common use as names for girls. However, Sabrina and Isla were both originally river names, Tara comes from the Tara (hill) in County Meath and Lorraine and Chantal have been borrowed directly from French places. The name Beverley shows just how complicated the story can be: it began life as a West Yorkshire place name, was carried to America as a surname, became a place name once more as the fashionable Beverly Hills, Hollywood, then spread back to Britain as a given name after it became very popular with American parents.

Film and Fiction

Many families borrow the names of a favourite book or film characters for their children and a long-running television series, a major new play or block-buster movie can launch a long-neglected or completely new name into fashion.

Gone With the Wind, one of the greatest box-office successes of all time, made Melanie very popular, introduced Bonnie as a given name and gave a boost to Ashley, Brent and Brett, though the name of the heroine, Scarlett, proved a little too exotic for most parents and is seldom used. In the 1940s the film *Laura* and the heroine of *Brief Encounter*, Laura Jesson, revived a name which had fallen into disuse and is now once again a favourite. Tammy only came into its own as an independent name after a popular series of films began with *Tammy and the Bachelor* in 1957. In the 1960s many baby girls were called Maria after the main characters in *West Side Story* and *The Sound of Music* and quite a few Benjamins owe their name to the hero of *The Graduate*. Perry, Jason and Darrin are boys' names which owe their popularity to 1960s TV series: *Perry Mason, Jason King* and *Bewitched* respectively.

Writers were influencing the choice of children's names long before films and television arrived. Some personal names were used for the first time in novels and poetry: Charles Dickens called the heroine of *Great Expectations* Estella, William Thackeray used Clive as the main character of *The Newcomes* and the Tudor poet Henry Howard, Earl of Surrey, wrote love poems to Geraldine.

Authors in search of new and different names for their characters come up with some interesting inventions of their own. Jonathan Swift, writing a poem about a friend, Esther Vanhomrigh, took the first three letters of her surname, added 'essa' a pet form of Esther, and produced Vanessa, and Fulke Greville, looking for an unusual name for his love poems, rearranged the letters of Mary to come up with Myra. Amanda was one of the decorative names first used by 18th century playwrights and novelists and though others, like Clarinda and Florinda, had little appeal for ordinary parents and soon faded out, Amanda lasted well and in more modern times took a new lease of life when Noël Coward used it in *Private Lives*. Marie Corelli, a well-known 19th century novelist, based Thelma on a Greek word meaning 'will' and J. M. Barrie made up Wendy for the little girl in *Peter Pan* because a friend's child nicknamed him 'Fwendie'.

Foreign Names

Names have never been limited by national boundaries and many of our favourites are originally foreign names which we have now made our own, so that they have lost any obvious links with the countries they came from originally. Established examples of this phenomenon are the Greek Philip and Irene or the Hebrew Daniel and Ruth.

Other foreign names are more recent imports which catch the ear of parents who are looking for something that is just a little unusual or exotic. From Scandinavia come vigorous names like Axel and Olaf for boys, Freya, Helga, Ingrid and Dagmar for girls, as well as Astrid and Magnus, both from the Norwegian royal family. From Spain come softer, flowing, more glamorous names like Benita, Carmen, Dolores and Elvira for girls, and boys' names such as Manuel and Ramon. German names are also popular, with boys' names like Bruno, Karl, Leopold, Rupert or Otto which have a forceful, masculine sound.

In the late 1960s and 1970s, following the epic film of Boris Pasternak's *Doctor Zhivago* and the television adaptation of Tolstoy's *War and Peace*, there was a minor vogue in Russian names like Natasha and its pet form, Tasha. Tamara, Tanya and Sonya were also widely used.

Over the past 100 years we have borrowed scores of French names, most of them for girls. Many parents like the pretty feminine ring of Arlette, Madeleine, Yvonne and Yvette and the more unusual Angelique, Chantal, Désirée and Yolande. The cadence of names like Danielle, Gabrielle and Michelle has been so popular that parents sometimes invent variations like Rachelle and Murielle, just to get a particular Continental sound. Most parents seem to find French names too 'fancy' for boys. Louis did quite well early in the 1900s, helped by the popularity of writer Robert Louis Stevenson, but was fast overtaken by the feminine Louise, which has remained popular throughout the years.

Foreign pet forms can sometimes give an unusual new look to a well-known name that has perhaps become regarded as rather ordinary. For instance, the German Greta comes from Margaret, the French Adèle from Adelaide and Anne seems to have diminutives all around the world: Annette in France, Annika in Sweden, Anouska in Russia, Anita in Spain.

Some names are truly international so that different languages have their own versions, which provide a fruitful field for parents who want something just that little bit different. Antony is Anton in German and Russian and Antonio in Spanish and Italian; Margaret is Marguerite in French, Margareta in German and Margarita in Spanish. Catherine is Caterina in Italian, Catriona in Gaelic, Karen in Danish and Karin in Swedish. John probably has the biggest score, with numerous foreign versions including Jan in Polish and Czech, Johan in Dutch, Sean in Gaelic, Ivan in Russian and Hans in German.

Saints' Names

Parents used to name their children after saints because they thought that along with the name would come the saintly attributes of piety, humility and compassion, though this could not always be guaranteed to happen! They also felt that the saints would be bound to take their young namesakes under their special protection. This tradition is not so popular nowadays but is still quite common amongst Catholic families.

Some of the most lasting and best-known names are those of the apostles, the most popular being John, James, Paul and Peter – and countless babies owe their names to the patron saints of England, Scotland, Ireland and Wales. George was the great soldier hero, one of the most famous of the early martyrs who, according to legend rescued a maiden by slaying a dragon, so that thousands of admirers were subsequently led to baptism. Andrew was the Galilean fisherman and brother of Saint Peter. Andrew was the first of the apostles called to follow Christ. Patrick was kidnapped by Irish raiders as a child and, though he later escaped to France, he returned to Ireland to preach the gospel. David was the son of a Welsh chief who presided over a strict order of monks.

A few saints, especially those whose stories include highly-coloured legends, have always been particular favourites with namesakes in every generation. St Christopher, whose image appears on so many lucky charms and medallions, was said to be a giant who carried the Christ-child across a ford, almost sinking beneath the weight of the whole world. St Nicholas, patron saint of children, was a 4th century bishop of Asia Minor whose good deeds included providing dowries of gold for several young girls to save them from prostitution. He is traditionally responsible for filling Christmas stockings because of the ancient custom of giving presents

14

on his feast day. Another well-loved saint is St Francis of Assisi who came from a rich family but chose to give up luxury and comfort to live a life of poverty and hard work, helping the needy.

The name of St Catherine, the patron saint of teachers and students, was famous throughout England in the Middle Ages, as her cult spread far and wide. Catherine was a high-born lady of Alexandria who was martyred because she refused to worship idols on the command of the emperor. Catherine has remained a particularly well-used name over the centuries. Irish families have always had a great fondness for St Brigid, the abbess of the country's first relgious community for women.

Namesakes of the saints are often children born on feast days, for instance: February 1, St Brigid; March 1, St David; March 17, St Patrick; April 23, St George; April 25, St Mark the Evangelist; May 16, St Brendan; June 29, St Peter and St Paul; July 1, St Mary Magdalene; September 21, St Matthew; September 29, St Michael and All Angels; October 4, St Francis of Assisi; October 18, St Luke; November 30, St Andrew.

Finally, the last thing to remember about selecting the perfect name is – don't rush! – a hasty choice may be regretted in later years. Deciding on a suitable name for your child is very important, so just take your time and enjoy choosing.

Aaron is a Biblical name – Aaron was the brother of Moses. Believed to be Egyptian in origin, it is increasing in popularity in recent years. A modern spelling is Aron.

Abbey and **Abbie** see **Abigail**

Abe see **Abraham**

Abel may be derived from the Hebrew word for 'breath' or 'son'. Though uncommon, it is still occasionally used.

Abigail comes from the Hebrew meaning 'father rejoices' and, in the Old Testament, was the name of King David's wife. It was popular among the Puritans in the 17th century and has been back in fashion over the past few years. Short forms include Abby, Abbey, Abbie and Gail.

Abraham comes from the Hebrew word for 'father'. It has remained popular in the USA since the time of President Abraham Lincoln. The most popular short form is Abe. The name is not so common in Britain.

Ada may come from a German word for 'noble' and was very popular in Victorian times.

Adam stems from the Hebrew for 'red', and was used for the colour of the skin. In the Old Testament, it was the name of the first man that God created on earth. It was widespread in the Middle Ages and many surnames (e.g. Adams, Adcock, Atkins) came from it. Pop star Adam Faith made it fashionable in the 1960s and it has remained popular ever since.

Adèle is the French pet form of the once-popular Adelaide meaning 'nobility' and was rediscovered by British parents quite recently. Modern spelling variations are Adell and Adelle.

Adrian comes from the Latin name *Adrianus*, describing a man from the town of Adria. The first English pope, Nicholas Breakspear, became Adrian IV but the name only became popular 30 or 40 years ago.

Adriana see **Adrienne**

Adrienne is the French feminine form of Adrian which proved far more popular in Britain than Adriana. Alternative spellings are Adriene and Adrianne; Adria is sometimes used.

Agatha comes from the Greek 'good'. St Agatha was a martyr in the 3rd century who is looked on as a protector against fire. Aggie is a short form.

Agnes comes from the Greek meaning 'pure' and for 400 years, from the Middle Ages onwards, it was one of the most frequently used first names. In recent years it has been more popular with Scottish than with English parents. Pet forms are Aggie and Nessie; in Wales Agnes has turned into Nesta and the Spanish form is Inez.

Aidan is an ancient Irish name from a word meaning 'fire'.

Aileen see **Eileen**

Aimée is the French version of Amy, and is becoming popular in its own right.

Al see **Albert** and **Alfred**

Alan was the name of an early Welsh and Breton saint and its meaning is uncertain; possibly 'rock' or 'harmony'. It was common in the Middle Ages and gave rise to many surnames (e.g. Alen, Allan, Alleyn). It had a big boost in the 1950s from the fame of actor Alan Ladd. Another well-known Alan is the playwright Alan Bennett. Alternative spellings are Allen, Allan, Allin and Alyn;

the Welsh use Alun. Alana is a feminine version.

Albert comes from the Old German *Adalbert*, meanig 'noble' and 'bright', and became enormously popular in the 19th century when Queen Victoria married Prince Albert. It has been one of the staple royal forenames ever since, though it has gone out of fashion in recent years. Pet names are Bert, Bertie and Al. The feminine versions are Alberta and Albertine, which is also the name of a climbing rose.

Aldous is derived from the Old German word meaning 'old' and has been used since the 13th century.

Alec is a shortened form of Alexander which is well known in its own right.

Alessandra is the Italian spelling of the feminine version of Alexander, and gave rise to the short form, Sandra. Alessia is another version.

Alethea is from an ancient Greek word meaning 'truth'.

Alexander stems from the Greek, meaning 'defender of men', and was made world-famous in the 3rd century BC by Alexander the Great. It is specially popular with Scottish parents though it is favoured throughout Britain. Shortened forms are Alex, Alix, Alick and Sandy, which are also used as independent names.

Alexandra is the feminine form of Alexander and was first used in England in the 13th century, though it only became popular after 1863 when the Prince of Wales married Alexandra of Denmark. It has been a popular royal name ever since. Variations include Alexandrina, Alexandria, Alexina and, in the last few years, Alix and Alexa.

Alexis comes from the Greek meaning 'helper' or 'defender' and began as a boy's name, but is now more used for girls.

Alf and **Alfie** see **Alfred**

Alfred means 'elf-counsel' in Anglo-Saxon; in early English history elves were regarded as powerful spirits of nature. Alfred the Great made the name famous but it later disappeared to come back into fashion in the late 18th and 19th centuries. Pet forms are Al, Alf, Alfie and Fred.

Alice has a long and complicated history; the original Greek means 'of a noble kind'. By the 18th century it was considered a country name but it came back in fashion after the publication of Lewis Carroll's *Alice in Wonderland* in 1865. Variations are Alicia, Alissa, Alisha and Alys.

Alicia see **Alice**

Alick see **Alexander**

Alison comes from Ailis, the Scots version of Alice, and has always been well liked in Scotland, although it was very popular in England in the 17th century. Since the 1930s it has overtaken Alice in popularity as a whole. The short form is Allie and alternative spellings include Allison and Alysanne.

Alistair is the phonetic spelling of Alasdair, the Gaelic version of Alexander (see page 18). Other variations like Alastair, Alister and Alisdair are used, but nowadays Alistair is the most popular form. The name is more commonly used in Scotland than in the rest of Britain. Broadcaster Alistair Cooke and writer Alistair MacLean are two of the best-known bearers of the name.

Allegra comes from Italy and means 'happy and cheerful'.

Alma is probably derived from the Latin word meaning 'kind' but may be from the Celtic for 'all good', the Hebrew for 'maiden' or the Spanish and Italian for 'soul' or 'spirit'. It is also the Russian name of a place that became known during the Crimean War, and it was at about that time that the name enjoyed its greatest popularity.

Alun see **Alan**

Alvin means 'noble friend' in German, and may be a version of Alwyn, which is still used in Wales.

Amanda comes from the Latin, meaning 'lovable'. Restoration dramatists used it along with other pretty inventions but it only became fashionable this century. The short form is Mandy, which has been popular with parents as an independent name over the past 20 years or so and is now seen as often as the full name from which it is derived.

Amber is a jewel name that was used in the 19th century and then faded out of fashion. The publication of the best-seller *Forever Amber* in the 1940s gave it a new lease of life.

Ambrose comes from the Greek meaning 'immortal' and though it has never been particularly fashionable it has been used for 300 years. Emrys is the Welsh form.

Amos means 'carried' in Hebrew and was the name of one of the Old Testament prophets. It was used regularly up to the end of the last century but it is now more unusual.

Amy derives from the Old French and means 'loved'. It was very fashionable towards the end of the 19th century, then went out of favour for two generations before becoming popular again with young parents. Amy was one of the four girls in *Little Women* and the name has always been popular in the USA. Variations are Amey, Amie and the French form Aimée.

Anastasia comes from the Greek for 'resurrection' and is a familiar name in Russia. Stacey is a shortened form now popular in English-speaking countries.

Andrea is the feminine form of Andrew (see below), first used in Britain in the 17th century and more popular in Scotland than in England. Variations include Andria, Andrina, Andrianna, Drena and Rena as well as the French form Andrée.

Andrew comes from the Greek meaning 'manly' and was the name of the first apostle. St Andrew is the patron saint of Scotland and Russia, so the name is popular in both countries. By the 1970s it was one of the most frequently used boys' names in English-speaking countries and has been a special favourite in Britain since Prince

Andrew was born in 1960. Diminutives are Andy and Drew, both used as forenames in their own right.

Andy see **Andrew**

Angela stems from the Greek meaning 'messenger', and began as the feminine form of the boy's name Angel, which has now disappeared. It has been frequently used all over the English-speaking world in recent years. The pet form is Angie and variations include Angelina, Angelica, and Angelique.

Angharad is a Welsh name and means 'very much loved'.

Angus is from the Gaelic word meaning 'unique choice' and was originally popular in Ireland, though it is now considered a Scottish name. Sir Angus Ogilvy, husband of Princess Alexandra, has kept the name in the public eye.

Anita is the Spanish form of Ann (see below) which became popular in the 1950s. Two well-known modern bearers of the name are singer Anita Harris and businesswoman Anita Roddick.

Ann(e) comes from the Hebrew name Hannah (see page 60), meaning 'grace', and was one of the top favourites with British parents for 300 years, until the middle of the last century. Six queens of England were called Anne and the name had a new boost after the birth of the Princess Royal in 1950. Nowadays it is more often used as a middle name. Pet forms are Annie and Nan. Annette is the French diminutive form with its variants of Annet, Annett and Annetta.

Anna is the Greek and Latin form of Hannah, and the forerunner of Ann(e). It was popular in Britain in the 18th century and is now enjoying a revival.

Annabel is another form of Amabel, which comes from the Latin and means 'lovable'. It has been specially well liked north of the border since the 14th century when Annabel Drummond was the mother of Scotland's King James I. Variations include Anabel, Annabelle and Annabella.

Annemarie, a linking of Anne and Marie (see pages 21 and 85), is a name which has only come into fashion over the past 30 years. Annamaria is a variation and both can be used with or without a hyphen between the two names.

Annette see **Ann**

Anthea comes from the Greek word meaning 'flowery' and was one of the titles of the goddess Hera in ancient Greece. It was first used as a girl's name by the 17th century poets and was in vogue earlier this century.

Anthony is from a Roman family name which may mean 'priceless'. The most popular spelling used to be Antony but nowadays parents seem to like Anthony better. St Antony, disciple of St Francis of Assisi and rescuer of lost property, has helped to keep the name in regular use and famous actors Anthony Perkins, Sir Anthony Quayle and Anthony Andrews have boosted its popularity. The short form is Tony.

Antonia is the feminine form of Antony (see above) and has been appearing more often on birth certificates over the past decade. A variation is the French form Antoinette and pet names are Toni or Tony and Tonya or Tonia; the last two sometimes used in their own right. Antonia Fraser, the historian, is a well-known bearer of the name.

April is the name of the month, first used as a forename early this century. The French form is Avril.

Arabella or Arabelle was first known in Scotland in the 13th century, but its meaning is not known. Bella and Belle are pet forms.

Archibald is derived from an Old German word meaning 'truly bold'. It has long been popular in Scotland. Archie is the short form.

Arlene may come from a Gaelic word meaning 'pledge' but its origins are obscure. It appeared for the first time in the 19th century as Arline and variations are Arleen, Arlyne and Arlena. The name is more commonly used in Scotland than in the rest of Britain.

Arnold stems from the Old German, meaning 'eagle-power'. It was first used in England after the Norman invasion as Arnaud but it faded from use and only came back into fashion in the late 19th century. The usual pet names are Arn and Arny.

Art see **Arthur**

Arthur might be from the Celtic word for 'bear', though its origins are not really known. It was made famous in the legend of King Arthur and his Knights of the Round Table and in the last century many boys were christened after the great military hero Arthur Wellesley, Duke of Wellington. Art is the short form.

Asa is a boy's name that comes from the Hebrew for 'healer'.

Ashley started off as a surname coming from the Anglo-Saxon for an 'ash-wood' and has only been used as a first name for a little over 100 years. It had a big boost from the film *Gone With The Wind*, in which one of the heroes is called Ashley. An alternative spelling is Ashleigh.

Athena comes from the Greek goddess of the same name and also from the city of Athens.

Aubrey finds its roots in the Old German word meaning 'elf-ruler' and the de Vere family brought it to England with the Norman Conquest. British parents only began using it with any frequency as a boy's name about 80 years ago.

Audrey started as a pet form of Ethelreda, which came from the Old English meaning 'noble strength'. It was going through its most popular phase when actress Audrey Heburn was born in 1929. Variations are Audra, Audree and Audria.

Aurora comes from Latin meaning 'golden dawn'. It became well known as it was the name of the princess in the ballet *Sleeping Beauty*.

Austin was originally a shortening of Augustine, stemming from the Latin word meaning 'venerable'. Though St Augustine was the founder of the Christian church in England and the first Archbishop of Canterbury, the English preferred their own shortened version of his name. Other variations are Austen, Austyn or Ostin and, in Wales, Awstin.

Avis is a girl's name brought to Britain by the Normans. It means 'refuge in war'. An alternative spelling is Avice.

Avril see **April**

Azura is Italian and means 'blue skies'.

B

Babette is a French name which is a diminutive form of Elizabeth.

Barbara derives from the Greek meaning 'strange' or 'foreign' and was originally written in English as Barbary. It came back into favour along with other medieval names at the beginning of this century. Abbreviations are Bab, Babs or Barbie and it is sometimes spelt Barbra. Famous modern name-bearers are the politician Barbara Castle and the actress Barbra Streisand.

Barnaby is the modern version of Barnabas, from the Hebrew meaning 'son of consolation', the name of the apostle who joined St Paul on his missionary journeys. It has never been a common name but has become more popular in recent years. Pet names are Barn or Barney.

Barry comes from an Irish word meaning 'spear' and was originally used only in Ireland. English parents seem to have adopted the name from Welsh and Scottish place names.

Bartholomew derives from the Hebrew meaning 'son of the furrow', probably a name originally given to a ploughman. It was common in the Middle Ages and led to surnames such as Bates, Bartlett and Batty. Short forms include Barty, Bartle and Tolly.

Basil comes from the Greek word meaning 'kingly'. The crusaders brought it to England and it was popular in the 19th century.

Bathsheba comes from Hebrew and means 'seventh child'.

Beatrice, which used to be spelt Beatrix, comes from the Latin meaning 'bringer of joy'. It was used for heroines by Dante,

Shakespeare and Thackeray. As it was the name chosen by Queen Victoria for her youngest daughter, the Duchess of York was following a royal tradition when she gave her first child the name in 1988. Nicknames are Bee, Bea, Beattie and Trixie.

Becky is a contraction of Rebecca, but considered as a name on its own. Thackerary used the name for Becky Sharp, the charming schemer in *Vanity Fair*.

Belinda is probably linked with the Old German word for 'serpent' but its origin is uncertain. It only came into use in England in the early 18th century.

Bella is the Italian for 'beautiful' and the usual short form of Isabella and Arabella. Belle means 'beautiful' in French.

Ben see **Benjamin**

Benedict means 'blessed' and stems from Latin. Surnames such as Benson and Bennett come from its frequent use in the Middle Ages. Bennet was one of the older variations and Shakespeare used it as Benedick. Nowadays it is mainly used by Roman Catholic families.

Benjamin comes from the Hebrew meaning 'son of the right hand' and the right hand was traditionally linked with strength. As the name of Jacob's beloved son in the Bible it was popular with the Puritans in the 17th century. Last century it received a boost through the popularity of Prime Minister Benjamin Disraeli and the name has recently come back into favour again. Pet forms are Ben, Benjy and Benny.

Bennet see **Benedict**

Berenice comes from the Greek meaning 'bringer of victory', and has been used in Britain since the 16th century. Bernice is the modern version and the short forms are Berny, Berry and Bunny.

Bernard comes from two Old German words meaning 'bear' and 'stern' or 'brave' and was made famous by St Bernard of Clairvaux and the saint who gave his name to St Bernard dogs. Victorian parents liked the name and it was popular in the first half of this century. Bernie is the short form, and occasionally Barney.

Bernadette is the French feminine form of Bernard (see page 26), made famous by St Bernadette of Lourdes. Other versions are Bernardette, Bernadine and Bernette.

Bertram comes from the Old German for 'bright raven'. The French version, Bertrand, means 'bright shield'. The names became merged because of the similar sound. The name came to England at the time of the Norman Conquest and enjoyed greatest popularity in the 19th century.

Beryl comes originally from the Sanskrit name for a precious stone. It only came in as a first name about 100 years ago when jewel names were fashionable.

Bess, like Bessie, is a popular shortened form of Elizabeth.

Beth is a shortened form not only of Elizabeth but also the Old Hebrew name Bethia.

Bethany is a biblical name and becoming increasingly popular.

Bettina is derived from Elizabeth, but is used as a name in its own right.

Betty is a form of Elizabeth that was very popular in the 1920s. Bette is an alternative spelling.

Beverley is from a surname originally taken from the place name meaning 'beaver stream'. It was first used as a boy's name (for example, writer Beverley Nichols) but in recent years has become popular as a girl's name in the USA – where it is usually spelt Beverly – and spread to England.

Bianca comes from the Italian word for 'white'. Bianca Jagger, ex-wife of Rolling Stone Mick Jagger, has kept the name in the public eye over the past few years.

Blair is taken from the Scottish surname which means 'flat land' and has been used as a boy's forename in modern times.

Blake is a surname coming from 'black', applied to a dark complexion, which has been used as a personal name only recently. It is less well known in England than in the USA.

Blanche comes from the French word for 'white'. It was first used in England in the 14th century and was one of the romantic-sounding girl's names popular in late Victorian times.

Bonnie see **Bonita**

Bonita comes from the Latin for 'good' and the Spanish for 'pretty'. Bonnie is the short form which has come to be used as an individual name since characters of that name featured in the films *Gone With The Wind* and *Bonnie and Clyde*.

Boris is a Russian name that means 'fight'. The actor Boris Karloff made it popular in English-speaking countries.

Boyd comes from the Celtic for 'yellow', probably describing colour of hair. It is a well-established Scottish font name.

Bradley is taken from a place name which originally meant 'wide clearing' and American and Australian parents use it more than the British. The usual abbreviations are Brad and Bradd.

Brenda comes from the Old Norse word for 'sword'. At first it was a Scottish name but became widespread after Sir Walter Scott used the name for one of his heroines. Victorian parents took a liking to it and it stayed popular up to the middle of this century.

Brendan probably derives from the Celtic meaning 'dweller by the beacon'. It was made famous by the 6th century Irish saint and parents have rediscovered it in recent years. Other spellings are Brandon and Brendon.

Brent is a place name originally meaning 'high' and has been used as a boy's name only recently.

Brett was originally a surname from the Latin meaning 'a Breton' and parents have adopted it as a forename for boys over the past 10 years or so.

Brian is an old Celtic name which may mean 'hill' or 'strength' and has always been widespread in Ireland because of the hero-king Brian Boru. Its use faded out quite early but came back into fashion this century. Other spellings are Bryan and Bryon and it sometimes becomes a girl's name as Brianne.

Bridget comes from the Celtic for 'the high one' or 'the august one'. It was made famous by the much-loved Irish saint who died in 523 and for hundreds of years was one of the commonest Irish names, later popular in Scotland. Other spellings are Brigid, Brigit and Bridgett and pet names are Biddy and Bridie.

Briony is one of the plant names that became popular with the Victorians. The dancer Briony Brind is a modern bearer of the name, which may also be spelt Bryony.

Bronwen means 'white breast' in Welsh and is often used as Bronwyn. It has always been far more popular in Wales than in the rest of Britain.

Bruce comes originally from a French place name probably meaning 'brushwood thicket' and came to Britain as a surname with the Norman Conquest. Scottish parents began using it as a given name less than 100 years ago and its popularity spread.

Bryn stems from the Welsh word for 'hill' and has only been used as a first name, mainly by Welsh parents, in recent years.

Bunty is a pet name coined from a stage production at the beginning of the century.

Caitlin is a Welsh form of Catherine.

Calanthea has its origins in Greece and means 'as beautiful as the flowers'.

Calista is also Greek in origin and means 'fairer than all other women'.

Calvin comes from the Latin for 'bald' and has been used as a boy's name since the time of the 16th century religious reformer of that name.

Cameron is a Scottish surname which means 'crooked stream' and has only recently been used as a given name, usually by Scottish parents.

Camilla comes from the Latin name for a noble attendant at services or sacrifices. It was quite fashionable after the publication of Fanny Burney's novel *Camilla* in the late 18th century and the success of the 1930s Greta Garbo film *Camille* gave the alternative spelling a boost.

Campbell derives from the Gaelic meaning 'crooked mouth' and was used only as a surname until this century when Scottish parents in particular adapted it as a forename. It is not used to a great extent in the rest of Britain.

Candice is derived from the title of Ethiopian queens. It has been used since the 17th century. The actress Candice Bergen has brought it to notice in modern times. An alternative spelling is Candace, and Candy is a pet form.

Cara means 'dear', from the Latin, and 'friend' from the Celtic. It has been increasing in popularity and is sometimes spelt Kara.

Carina is an unusual modern name for a girl, from the Italian for 'dear'.

Carl comes from the Old German meaning 'a man', which gave us the English name Charles (see page 33). Over the past 30 years the Germanic form Carl, often spelt Karl, has become fashionable in England.

Carla is the feminine version of Carl (see above) which became popular with American parents long before its use spread to Britain. It is sometimes spelt Karla. Carly is a modern variation. Singer Carly Simon has made the variation popular.

Carlo is the Italian, Carlos the Spanish equivalent of Charles.

Carmel is from Hebrew meaning 'garden'.

Carmen means 'song' in Latin, and is familiar from the name of the heroine of Bizet's opera.

Carol is a form of Charles, and can be used as a boy's name though is usually given to a girl. Alternative spellings are Caryl, Carroll and Carole. The film actresses Carole Lombard and Carroll Baker made the name extremely popular. The name has remained constantly popular in recent times.

Caroline began as the feminine of Carlo, the Italian version of Charles (see page 33). It was a great favourite in the 18th century, when George II's queen was called Caroline, and came back into the forefront of fashion this century. It also appears as Carolyn or Carolyne and the pet forms are Carrie or Caro.

Cary was originally a surname, possibly meaning 'fort' and only became well known as a boy's first name after the actor Archibald Leach rechristened himself Cary Grant and very quickly rose to fame. Scottish parents sometimes use it as a girl's name. It may be spelt Carey.

Casey means 'valorous', from a Celtic word, and can be used for boys and girls.

Casper see **Jasper**

Cassandra comes from the Greek for 'helper of men' and is one of the famous names of mythology, belonging to the prophetess who foretold the fall of Troy. It is an old-established name in Britain, most often used in the 17th century. Short forms are Cass or Cassie.

Catherine derives from the Greek word meaning 'pure' and has been popular as an English given name for 800 years. Catherine is the favourite spelling, though the older forms are Katherine or Katharine and there are all sorts of variations, including Cathryn, Catherina and Catrine, which can all begin with a 'K'. Cathleen or Kathleen is the Irish version, Catriona the Scottish and Catrin the Welsh. Shortenings include Cathy, Kate and Katie.

Catriona is a Scottish variant of Catherine and the title of a novel by Robert Louis Stevenson. It is still much favoured in Scotland.

Cecil is derived from a family name of Ancient Rome. It came into favour in the 19th century when Cecil Rhodes achieved fame.

Cecilia is the feminine form of Cecil. The 2nd century St Cecilia is the patroness of music. The name came into Britain with the Norman Conquest and has many forms, such as Cecile, Cecily and Cicely. Cissie is a short form.

Cedric has a Victorian air about it, probably because it was the name of the hero of *Little Lord Fauntleroy*, but its meanings and origins are unclear.

Celia stems from Latin and means 'heavenly'. The early spelling was Caelia, the form used in Ancient Rome and it was popular here in the 18th and 19th centuries, along with Cecilia.

Chad was the name of a monk who became bishop of the Mercians in the 7th century. Its meaning is uncertain but could be 'warrior'. It has been used sparingly over the centuries but there has been more interest in the name during the past 20 years and a well-known bearer is the Rev Chad Varah, founder of the Samaritans.

Chantal is a French girl's name derived from the word for 'song'. It is sometimes spelt Chantelle.

Charles comes from the Old German word meaning 'a man' and has been a favourite royal name since it was adopted by the House of Stuart in the 17th century. Famous men like Charles de Gaulle, the actors Charlie Chaplin and Charles Bronson and, above all, Prince Charles, have helped keep the name popular. Pet names are Charlie, Charley, Chas, Carl, Karl and Chay.

Charlotte is the feminine of Carlo, Italian for Charles (see above) and became popular when George III married Charlotte Sophia in 1761. It fell out of favour early this century then staged a comeback over the past two decades. A variation is Carlotta and nicknames include Lottie, Lotty, Totty and Charlie.

Charmian comes from the Greek meaning 'joy' and was used by Shakespeare for one of Cleopatra's slaves in *Antony and Cleopatra*. Charmaine is a modern version which was the name of a popular song.

Chas see **Charles**

Chay strictly speaking is a short form of Charles, however it has also come into use as an individual name. The fame of lone yachtsman Chay Blyth, has helped to make it better known.

Cher comes from the French and means 'dearly loved'. It has grown in popularity recently due to the fame of actress and singer, Cher.

Cherry began as a pet form of Charity, which had been popular with the 17th century Puritans. It came into its own as an independent name along with the flower names favoured by the Victorians.

Cheryl is a modern name which comes from the Welsh word for 'love' and has been well used by parents in English-speaking countries in recent years. Variations include Cheryll and Cheralyn.

Chloe derives from the Greek word meaning 'a tender budding plant' and in the past was always more popular with poets than with parents but has been used increasingly in the last few years.

Christabel means 'fair follower of Christ' and comes from a combination of Greek and Latin. It was mainly used in the north before Coleridge's poem 'Christabel' spread its popularity in the early 19th century. Suffragette leader Christabel Pankhurst kept it in the public eye. Variations are Christabelle, Christobel and Christabella and the usual pet names are Chris, Chrissie and Christy.

Christian, from the Latin meaning 'following of Christ', was first used as a girl's name but John Bunyan gave it to the hero of *Pilgrim's Progress* in 1684 and since then it has normally been used for boys, with Christiana as the feminine form. It has come back into fashion in recent years. Prince Andrew's second name is Christian.

Christine began as Christina coming, like the boy's name Christian, from the Latin for 'follower of Christ' and in recent years it has increased in popularity. Variations include Christeen, Kristin and Kristina.

Christopher comes from the Greek meaning 'bearing Christ' and became well known through St Christopher, who was supposed to have carried the Christ-child across a river. It was out of favour in the last century, then stormed back into fashion in the 1900s, helped by A.A. Milne's character Christopher Robin. A variation is Kristopher and shortenings are Chris, Kris and Kit. Christy is a short form used in Ireland.

Cicely see **Cecilia**

Cindy is an abbreviation of Lucinda or Cynthia which has become popular as a name on its own.

Clara see **Clare**

Clare derives from the Latin word meaning 'bright' or 'clear' and has been one of the most fashionable names over the past few years. Although, it has been used regularly for around 700 years. Claire is the modern spelling and Clara was the popular version in Victorian times.

Clarissa replaced the Latin name Clarice and became well-liked after the publication of a novel of the same name in 1748 by Samuel Richardson.

Clark was originally a surname meaning 'clerk' or 'cleric'. It gained ground as an established first name through the fame of actor Clark Gable and still catches parents' imaginations through the hero of the *Superman* films, reporter Clark Kent.

Claudette and Claudine are both the French feminine forms of Claudius, which came from the Latin for 'lame'. They are more popular in modern times than the old-established name Claudia.

Claudia see **Claudette**

Cleo is strictly speaking the short form of Cleopatra, which means 'fame' or 'glory' in Greek. In modern times however, it has been used as a name in its own right, for example by the popular jazz singer Cleo Laine.

Clifford derives from a place name meaning 'ford at a slope'. It became a surname and was first used as a forename in the 19th century. These days it is usually shortened to Cliff and it gained in popularity through the publicity given to the popular singer Cliff Richard.

Clint see **Clinton**

Clinton comes from a place name meaning 'headland farm'. It is usually shortened to Clint and its use has been given a boost by actor Clint Eastwood.

Clive stems from a place name meaning 'cliff', which became a surname. British families living in India began using it as a given name after the founder of modern India, Sir Robert Clive.

Clyde is the name of a Scottish river which began to be used as a first name at the beginning of the century.

Colette is a pet French name, and that of the famous author of *Gigi*.

Colin was, in England, originally a pet name for Nicholas and became a first name in its own right around 700 years ago but in Scotland Colin came from Gaelic meaning 'young dog' or 'youth'. Variations are Colin and Colan. A famous modern bearer is cricketer Colin Cowdrey.

Colleen comes from the Irish for 'girl', and has only relatively recently been used as a first name.

Conan comes from the Old Celtic meaning 'high' and is best known in Ireland, though its use spread in the late 19th century through the fame of Sir Arthur Conan Doyle, creator of Sherlock Holmes.

Connie see **Constance**

Conrad has its origins in the Old German word meaning 'brave counsel'. Though it was the name of a 10th-century saint it was seldom used in Britain before the mid-19th century.

Constance traces its descent from the Latin word meaning 'constancy'. It has been used in Britain in various forms for hundreds of years: Custance in the Middle Ages, Constancy in the 17th century and Constantia in Victorian times. The pet form is Connie.

Cora may be derived from the Greek word for 'maiden'. It has only been in use for about 100 years and is more popular in the USA than in Britain.

Coral is one of the jewel names first used around 100 years ago and its variation is Coralie. A well-known bearer is actress Coral Browne.

Corinne comes from the Greek meaning 'maiden'. The older version is Corinna and among the other spellings are Corrinne and Correne. Corin is occasionally used as a boy's name, for example, the actor Corin Redgrave.

Cordelia is the name of the faithful daughter in Shakespeare's *King Lear* and has occasionally been used in recent years.

Cornelius is derived from a family name of Ancient Rome, and is occasionally used today. Cornel is a short form and the feminine equivalent is Cornelia.

Courtney is a French place name that is used for both boys and girls.

Craig was originally a surname, stemming from the Gaelic for 'crag' and only became a forename in recent years, quickly becoming a favourite.

Cressida is a classical girl's name from the Greek word for 'gold'.

Crispin means 'curly-haired', deriving from Latin, and was made famous by the 3rd-century patron saint of shoemakers. It had faded out of use by the 19th century but has caught the imagination of parents in recent times.

Crystal is one of the jewel names which were popular in the 19th century, and is sometimes used today in Scotland.

Curtis comes from the Old French word 'courteous' and is a surname which has often been used as a first name. The old spelling was Curteis.

Cynthia was one of the titles of the goddess Artemis because she was supposed to come from Mount Cynthos. It was popular with 16th century poets and with English parents earlier this century.

Cyril comes from the Greek meaning 'lord'. It was at its most popular in the 1920s, but has now gone out of fashion.

Cyrus comes from the Persian *kuru*, 'throne'. The Puritans adopted this name which occurs in the Old Testament.

Daisy, which comes from the Anglo-Saxon meaning 'day's eye', was one of the flower names popular in late Victorian times. In France the same name was Marguerite, so Daisy was also a pet form for Margaret.

Dale was a surname meaning 'valley', which has been used as a given name for 100 years or so. Its popularity was helped by the fame of the American writer Dale Carnegie and though it was originally used for boys and girls, it is now usually a male name. The name is more commonly used in America than it is in Britain.

Damian comes from the Greek and means 'one who tames'. It was the name of the 5th century patron saint of doctors but has only been popular with parents over the past 30 years or so. Variations are Damien, Damion and Damon.

Damon see **Damian**

Dana comes from the name of the Celtic goddess of fertility but has been used for both girls and boys, especially in the USA.

Daniel comes from the Hebrew meaning 'God is my judge', well known from the Biblical prophet who was thrown into the lion's den. It was in fashion with other Biblical names in the 17th century and in recent years has again turned into a top favourite. Shortened forms are Dan and Danny and famous bearers include the actor Danny Kaye and entertainer Danny la Rue.

Danielle is the French feminine form of Daniel (see above) which has been growing in popularity over recent years. Variations are Daniele, Daniela and Daniella.

Daphne means 'bay' or 'laurel' in Greek and was the name of a nymph loved by Apollo and turned into a bush by the gods as she ran away from him. It appeared in Britain only at the turn of the century and was kept in the public eye by author Daphne du Maurier. Nick-names are Daff and Daffy.

Darcy began as a surname, D'Arcy, which in turn came from a French place name, brought to England with the Norman Conquest. Darcy was originally used as a first name by Irish parents and its use spread to Britain.

Darren was a surname meaning 'dearly beloved', first used as a given name in the USA. British parents took a great liking to it and it has been very fashionable over the past 20 years. Variations include Darrin, Darran, Darryn and Darien.

Darryl comes from an Anglo-Saxon word meaning 'beloved' and was in vogue earlier this century in its various forms: Daryl, Darrell, Darrel, Darrol.

David means 'darling' and comes from the Hebrew. In the Bible it was the name of the boy who killed the giant Goliath and later became king of Israel and father of the great king Solomon. The 6th century patron saint of Wales and two Scottish kings were called David, so it was always a popular name with Welsh and Scottish parents and over the past 100 years it has been one of the top favourites all over Britain. Pet names are Dave and Davey. Welsh parents have often used Dafydd, shortened to Dai or Taffy.

Davina is a Scottish feminine form of David, which dates from the 17th century and has tended to oust the less popular Davida. Variations are Davinia and Davena.

Dawn is the English translation of the old-established name Aurora, the Latin name for 'dawn'. Aurora was in vogue in the 19th century, but since then Dawn has more or less taken over, having been popularized by novelists and short story writers.

Dean was originally a surname meaning 'valley', which stemmed from the Anglo-Saxon. It became well known through several famous Americans, such as the singer Dean Martin. Deana is sometimes used for girls.

Deanna is a variation on Diana popularized in the 1940s by singer Deanna Durbin.

Deanne is a version of the French Diane, and is pronounced with the emphasis on the first 'e'.

Deborah is the Hebrew word for 'bee' and later came to mean 'eloquence'. It was the name of a Biblical prophetess, and the 17th-century Puritans were fond of it. It came back into fashion in the middle of this century, with the shortened version, Debbie, used independently as a first name. Actresses Deborah Kerr and Debbie Reynolds helped its popularity. Variations include Debora and Debra.

Debra see **Deborah**

Dee started as a pet name for anyone whose name began with 'D' but is now used as a first name in its own right, particularly for girls, though it can be a boy's name.

Deirdre derives from the Old Celtic meaning 'the raging one' and though it is an ancient Irish name it has come into its own only since the early years of this century when two Irish writers, W.B. Yeats and J.M. Synge used it for their heroines. Since then it has been widely used in Britain.

Delia is another name for the Greek goddess Artemis and was a favourite of 17th century poets. The cookery writer Delia Smith has made it well known in the present day.

Della was originally a short form of Delia or Adela, but has become better known in its own right.

Delys could possibly come from an old Latin first name meaning 'delight', though its exact origins have never been fully discovered.

Denis came originally from the Greek name Dionysos, the god of wine and revelry and was used in the Middle Ages when it led to surnames such as Dennis, Dennison, Denny and Tennyson. It was particularly popular early this century, often spelt as Dennis, with the nicknames Den and Denny. Actor Dennis Waterman and politician Denis Healey have helped to keep the name in the public eye.

Denise is a name which, in its present form, was borrowed from France by British parents early this century. Like Denis (see above) it comes from a Greek name and girls in England were called by the original form of Denis as far back as the Middle Ages. Variations are Denyse and Denice.

Denzil was first a Cornish place name, Denzell, then a surname, then a given name. Denzil is the usual spelling, though there are variations such as Denzel and Denziel. Popular in the last century, the name has enjoyed a revival in recent years. Politician Denzil Davies has kept the name in the public eye.

Derek comes from the Old German word meaning 'ruler of the people'. It has been quite fashionable in its various forms, including Derrick, Deryk, Deryck, Rick and Ricky in this century. Actor Dirk Bogarde uses the Dutch form of the name.

Dermot is the English version of a Celtic name meaning 'free from envy'. The 12th century king of Leinster was called Dermot so it has always been well known in Ireland and is very popular with Irish parents today. Diarmid is the Gaelic version.

Desdemona was the tragic heroine in Shakespeare's *Othello*. The name is a beautiful one but not commonly used.

Desmond was originally an Irish surname meaning 'a man from south Munster' and was first used as a given name by Irish parents, then also by English parents around the turn of the century. The usual abbreviation is Des.

Diana was the Latin name for the moon goddess. French parents began using it as Diane in the 16th century and English parents anglicized the name. Diane came later and other variations are

Dianne and Deanna. The Princess of Wales has given the popularity of the name a boost in recent years.

Dick see **Richard**

Dinah is an ancient Biblical name, that of Jacob's daughter, and means 'judged'. It is not a variant of Diana.

Dion was originally the short form of Dionysos, the Greek god of wine, which also turned into Denis (see page 40).With the feminine version Dionne it is popular with families of West Indian origin.

Dirk see **Derek**

Dodie is a pet name derived from Dorothy which is occasionally used independently.

Dolores comes from a Spanish name used as a short form for *Maria de los Dolores*, 'Mary of the sorrows', one of the titles of the Virgin Mary. Before it became popular in the 1930s in Hollywood, it was only used in Roman Catholic countries. Pet forms are Lola and Lolita, sometimes used independently.

Dominic stems from the Latin word meaning 'belonging to the Lord' and has been used by Roman Catholic families since the 13th-century saint founded the Dominican order of friars. Recently it has become far more widely popular. A variation is Dominick and the French form Dominique is used for girls.

Don see **Donald**

Donald comes from the Gaelic meaning 'world-ruler' and six Scottish kings were called Donald. It has always been a favourite Highland name but has become popular with English parents. The pet form is Don and Donal is the well-used Irish version.

Donna comes from the Italian for 'lady' and is a recent arrival as a popular given name, first in America then in England. Madonna is a variant meaning 'my lady'.

Dora originated as a familiar form of Dorothy, then became used as an independent name in the 19th century, for example by Charles Dickens in *David Copperfield*.

Doreen is possibly derived from Dorothy although it is now regarded as a name in its own right.

Doris comes from a Greek place name and became very popular in Britain at the end of the 19th century.

Dorothy stems from the Greek meaning 'gift of God'. It was such a common name in the 16th and 17th centuries that it gave its pet form 'Doll' to a girls' favourite toy. Victorian parents preferred Dorothea but Dorothy came back into fashion early this century and gained popularity with the success of the film *The Wizard of Oz*. Pet forms, besides Doll, are Dolly, Dot, Dotty and Dodie.

Dougal was originally the Irish name for the Danes, from the Gaelic meaning 'dark stranger'. It became a surname and was later taken up by Scottish parents as a first name. It is now mainly used in the Highlands, with the variations Dugald and Dhugal.

Douglas derives from a Celtic place name taken from the Gaelic word meaning 'dark water' and became the surname of an important aristocratic Scottish family. By the 17th century it was used as a first name for both girls and boys. Now used only for boys, it was very popular in the middle of this century, boosted by the fame of the actor Douglas Fairbanks Jnr and the renowned pilot, war-hero Douglas Bader.

Drew comes from the Old French for 'sturdy' as well as being the pet name for Andrew (see page 20) and its use as a forename in its own right is fairly new.

Drusilla is derived from the family name of an Ancient Roman clan, and is a diminutive feminine form.

Duane began as a Celtic surname meaning 'black', later used as a first name and given a boost in recent years by the musician Duane Eddy. Variations include Dwane and Dwayne.

Dudley is an Old English place name meaning 'Duda's clearing', made famous as a surname by Robert Dudley, Earl of Leicester, in the reign of Queen Elizabeth I. It became well known as a first name about 100 years ago and has been kept in the public eye in recent years by the comedian Dudley Moore.

Duke is sometimes given as the short form of Marmaduke, but also taken from the title, especially in the USA, for example by jazz musician Duke Ellington.

Dulcie is a modern name stemming from Latin and meaning 'sweet'. It was in fashion in the early part of this century and a well-known bearer of the name is actress Dulcie Gray.

Duncan is an old Celtic name meaning 'brown soldier'. Two Scottish kings, one of them made world-famous by Shakespeare in *Macbeth*, were called Duncan and it has always been a well-used name in Scotland. English and Welsh parents adopted it quite recently. The name was given a boost recently by the popularity of Duncan Goodhew.

Dwight originally comes from the French name Diot. Its most famous holder has been the US President Dwight Eisenhower.

Dylan is the name of a legendary Welsh hero, the son of a sea-god and means 'son of the wave'. The poet Dylan Thomas made the name famous so that it is now used in both England and Wales.

Earl comes from the British title and is probably more popular in the United States than it is in Britain.

Eartha comes from Old English and means 'of the Earth'. It has been revived in recent years due to the fame of singer and T.V. personality Eartha Kitt.

Edgar comes from the Old English meaning 'prosperous spear' and was the name of the first publicly acknowledged King of England. It came into fashion in the 19th century when Sir Walter Scott used it as the name of his hero in *The Bride of Lammermoor*, then tended to fade out of use again. Shortenings are Ed and Eddie.

Edith is made up of two Old English words meaning 'rich' and 'war' and is a long-established first name, used well before the Norman Conquest. It was one of the most fashionable names in the late 19th century and pet forms are Eda, Ede and Edie. Actress Dame Edith Evans, poet Edith Sitwell and singer Edith Piaf are among famous 20th century bearers of the name.

Edmund is made up of two Old English words meaning 'happy' and 'protection'. It was made famous by two saints and two early kings of England, and has never fallen out of use. Edmond is a popular modern variation and the Irish forms Eamon or Eamonn have always been well used. Nicknames are Ed, Eddie, Ned, Ted or Teddie.

Edna appears as a first name in the Bible but its meaning is uncertain; some suggestions are 'rejuvenation' or 'delight'. English parents began using it about 200 years ago and it was very fashionable around the turn of the century.

Edward, like Edmund (see page 45), comes from the Old English words meaning 'happy' and 'protection', and parents have always preferred Edward. Short forms are plentiful – Ed, Eddie, Ned, Neddie, Ted, Teddy – and famous bearers include the composer Edward Elgar, ex-Prime Minister Edward Heath and actors Edward Fox and Edward Woodward.

Edwin stems from Old English meaning 'rich friend' and was a common name in the days before the Norman Conquest. It became fashionable again in Victorian times. It is sometimes used as Edwyn and can be shortened to Ed or Eddie. Edwina is the feminine version which has remained in use. The name was popular in the 1940s by Lady Edwina Mountbatten, Countess of Burma.

Eileen with its alternative spelling Aileen, is a Celtic name which seems to have become a substitute for Helen (see page 61). It became generally popular in Britain in the late 19th century, when Irish names were in fashion. Diminutives are Eily or Eiley.

Elaine is an old French form of Helen (see page 61) meaning 'the bright one' which appeared as a personal name in Britain only after Tennyson used it in his *Idylls of the King*.

Eleanor stems from a French version of Helen (see page 61) and came to Britain with Henry II's wife, Eleanor of Aquitaine, though it was Edward I's queen who made it popular. It is sometimes spelt Elinor and contractions include Nell, Nellie, Ella, Leonore and Leonora, several of them used as names in their own right.

Eli comes from the Hebrew word for 'height'. The Puritans brought it into use in the 17th century and some families still favour it, though it is not commonly used.

Eliot is a modern first name which can be traced back to the Hebrew name Elias. A well-known bearer is actor Elliott Gould.

Elise see **Elizabeth**

Elizabeth comes from the Hebrew meaning 'oath of God' and was already a royal name when Queen Elizabeth II made it one of the best-loved girls' forenames in Britain. It has been popular for so long that there are many short forms, including Bess, Beth, Betty, Elise, Eliza, Libby, Liz, Lisa, Lise, Lisette and Liza. An alternative spelling is Elisabeth and in Scotland it developed into Elspeth.

Ella comes from the Old German word for 'all' and was one of the Norman names which came to Britain at the time of the Conquest. It had a new lease of life when Victorian parents took it up along with other medieval names. Singer Ella Fitzgerald is one of the best-known bearers of the name.

Ellen is an early English form of Helen, though it has long been treated as an independent name. It is especially well liked in Scotland.

Ellis is an old French form of the Hebrew name Elias.

Elma is a shortened form of Gulielma, the Italian feminine form of William. It is more popular in the United States than in Britain.

Elmer is from an Anglo-Saxon word meaning 'noble, famous'.

Elroy is from the Latin, 'regal' and is also popular in France where it derives from the title 'the king'.

Elsa comes from two Old German words meaning 'noble maiden' and the Scottish version, now sometimes used by English parents, is Ailsa.

Elspeth see **Elizabeth**

Elton is an old English place name which means 'Ella's enclosure' and has been used as a font name only in modern times, given a boost in popularity by the singer Elton John.

Emily comes, with Amelia, from an Old German word meaning 'hard-working'. It was a great favourite in the 19th century, when one of the best-known bearers was the novelist Emily Brontë. Other popular versions are Emilia and Emilie and pet names are Em and Emmy.

Emma comes from Old German meaning 'universal' or 'all-embracing' and was made famous in Norman times when Queen Emma married Ethelred the Unready and later King Canute. It was brought back to public attention by Lord Nelson's mistress Emma Hamilton, and then by Jane Austen's novel *Emma*. In the past few years it has once again been a top favourite and is often shortened to Em.

Enid is a Welsh name meaning 'life' and became popular in the 19th century with the translation of the Arthurian legend in which the name appears.

Eric probably means 'ruler', coming from Old Norse, but its roots are uncertain. It was only generally accepted as a personal name in the 19th century. Variants include Rick and Ricky.

Erica is used as the feminine of Eric (see above) but it is also the English translation of the Latin name for 'heather' and Victorian parents, with their liking for flower and plant names, used it for this reason. Erika is an alternative spelling.

Erin, from the Gaelic meaning 'western isle', is a poetic name for Ireland which has only recently appeared as a first name.

Ernest is the anglicized form of the German name Ernst, meaning 'vigour'. Ernestine is the feminine form.

Errol is believed to be a corruption of the title 'earl' and used as a first name. The actor Errol Flynn made it famous.

Esme from the Latin for 'esteemed' was originally a boy's name used in Scotland but is now more likely to be given to girls.

Esmeralda is from the Spanish for 'Emerald'. It was made famous through the girl in Victor Hugo's *Hunchback of Notre Dame*.

Estelle probably comes from the Old French word for a 'star'. It became acceptable in the 19th century when Charles Dickens used it for the heroine of *Great Expectations*.

Esther comes from the Persian meaning 'star' and though it appears in the Old Testament it did not catch on as a given name until the 17th century when Biblical names were in fashion. Another version of the name is Hester and abbreviations are Etty, Hetty and Tessa. T.V. personality Esther Rantzen is a modern bearer of the name.

Ethan is a Hebrew boy's name meaning 'constancy', and is sometimes used in the USA. Ethan Allen was a prominent figure in the American War of Independence.

Ethel comes from the Anglo-Saxon word 'noble'. It was used as a prefix in names like Ethelred which are now almost extinct, but was revived in the short form by Thackeray with one of the characters in *The Newcomes*, published in 1855.

Eugene derives from Greek meaning 'born lucky' and four popes took the name. American parents have used it more often than the British and it is frequently shortened to Gene, as in the example of actor Gene Hackman.

Eunice comes from the Greek for 'happy victory'. It was used in England in the 17th century but has never been widely popular.

Eustacia is a feminine form of Eustace which has been little used, except by Thomas Hardy in *The Return of the Native*. Stacey is the modern variant.

Eva and **Eve** come from the Hebrew word for 'life' and, according to the Bible, this was the name given to the first woman on earth. In the Middle Ages parents used it for their daughters because they believed that it would ensure long life and it was fashionable in Victorian times. The pet form is Evie, and Ava is a variation.

Evan is the Welsh form of John (see page 72) meaning 'God is gracious', and has been used since about 1500.

Evelyn is an old German name of uncertain meaning. Its use as a forename for both girls and boys has been fairly widespread in

Britain since the 18th century. Eveline and Evelina are variations used only for girls.

Everard comes from an old German word meaning 'boar'. The Normans brought the name to England. Variations include Everett.

Everett see **Everard**

Ewan is probably derived from the Gaelic for 'youth'. It was once a common name in England but is now mainly used by Scottish parents.

Ezekiel is a Biblical name which comes from the Hebrew, 'God strengthens'.

Ezra, like Ezekiel, was a favourite with the Puritans in the 17th century. Another Biblical name, it means 'help'. The best-known modern example is the poet Ezra Pound.

Faith is one of the 'virtue' names which appealed so much to the Puritans. It was originally given to boys and girls and has survived as a girl's name, with Fay as a short form as well as an independent name.

Fanny is an abbreviation of Frances but has been used independently, though it is out of fashion now.

Faustina is from Latin and means 'good luck'.

Fay or Faye has disputed origins: it may be from the old word 'fay' meaning 'faith' or from the Old French meaning 'fairy'. It has only been used as a name since the turn of the century. Actress Faye Dunaway has helped to publicize it.

Felicia see **Felix**

Felicity originally comes from the Latin word meaning 'happiness' and the favoured early versions were Felice and Felicia. The Puritans then used the modern form Felicity as another of their 'virtue' names and the success of comedy actress Felicity Kendal has kept the name popular in recent years. Common pet forms include Flic, Fee and Fliss.

Felix stems from the Latin word meaning 'happy' and has a very distinguished pedigree, as the name borne by four popes and several saints, though it is rather uncommon today. Felicia is the feminine form.

Fenella is Gaelic in origin and means 'white shoulders'. Finola is a common variant.

Fergus is a Celtic name which means 'supreme choice' and is used mainly by Scottish parents or in Ireland, with the older spelling Feargus. The usual abbreviation is Fergie.

Fern comes from the plant of the same name and is more commonly used in the United States than it is in Britain.

Fiona comes from the Gaelic word for 'fair'. It only appeared as a given name at the turn of the century and has become fashionable over the past 20 years.

Finn is an Irish name, a short form of Finnbarr or Finbar, and best known as the giant Finn McCool of Irish legend.

Flora comes from the Latin for 'flowers'. After Flora Macdonald's heroism in the Jacobite rebellion the name was sure of its place as a favourite in Scotland.

Florence derives from the Latin for 'blooming' and became especially popular as a girl's name with the fame of Florence Nightingale. Short forms are Flo, Florrie and Flossie.

Floyd probably developed from the Celtic surname Lloyd (see page 81) meaning 'grey' or 'dark' when the English tried to pronounce the difficult 'll' sound. In Britain it is well liked by families of West Indian origin.

Francis and Frances stem from the Latin word meaning a 'Frenchman'. St Francis of Assisi made the name popular in the Middle Ages and it was used, with Frank as the shortened version, for both boys and girls but later Frances became the popular feminine form, with Francine and Francesca as variations. Pet names for girls are Fran, Francie and Frankie and for boys Frank and Frankie.

Frank and **Frankie** see **Francis**

Franklin comes from the Norman French for 'freeholder'. One of Chaucer's pilgrims in the *Canterbury Tales* was a franklin. The name became popular as a sign of respect to Benjamin Franklin, the American statesman.

Fraser has an uncertain origin but may come from the Old English for 'curly-haired'. It is an old-established Highland surname, only used as a first name over the past 50 years or so, mainly by Scottish parents. It is often spelt as Frazer.

Fred see **Alfred, Frederick**

Freda is an abbreviation of Winifred and of Frederica, sometimes spelt Frieda in the German way.

Frederick comes from two Old German words meaning 'peaceful ruler'. It was one of the most popular boy's names in the 19th century. Other spellings are Fredric or Fredrick, shortened to Fred or Freddie. It has been publicized by modern bearers such as the cricketer Fred Trueman, the comedian Freddie Starr and the novelist Frederick Forsyth. Feminine forms are Freda, Frederica and Frederique.

G.

Gabriel derives from the Hebrew for 'man of God' and, in the Bible, it was the name of the Archangel who told the Virgin Mary that she was to give birth to Christ. The feminine form is Gabrielle and shortened versions are Gabe and Gabby.

Gail is a modern addition to the general stock of British names and was originally a diminutive of Abigail (see page 16) meaning 'father rejoices'.

Gareth has obscure origins but may be from the Welsh meaning 'gentle' and has been used as a given name since the 16th century. The shortened modern version is Garth. Once used mainly in Wales, it has become widely used over the past few years, helped by the popularity of actor Gareth Hunt.

Garth see **Gareth**

Garfield means 'field of spears', stemming from Anglo-Saxon and was used first as a surname. It was popularized by the cricketer Sir Garfield Sobers and is well liked by families of West Indian origin.

Garnet originates from the precious stone of the same name.

Gary was originally an abbreviation of the name Garret, the ancient version of Gerard (see page 56) meaning 'spear-brave', and brought into the forefront of fashion in the US and Britain by the actor Gary Cooper. Garry is an alternative spelling.

Gasper see **Jasper**

Gavin traces its history to Gawain, from the Welsh meaning 'little hawk' and was the name of one of King Arthur's distinguished knights. Gavin is the Scottish version and is now popular with the varying spellings of Gavan, Gaven and Gavyn.

Gay means 'lively' in French but could come from the Greek meaning 'earth goddess'.

Gaynor developed from Guenevere, the name of King Arthur's wife who fell in love with Lancelot. It means 'fair lady'. Other spellings are Gayner and the Welsh form Gaenor.

Gemma is Italian for 'gem' and has been used recently as a personal name, becoming quite a favourite with British parents. Another spelling is Jemma.

Gene see **Eugene**

Genevieve is a French name but its origins and meaning are uncertain. The 5th century St Genevieve is the patron saint of Paris, so the name has always been popular with French families. In Britain it is still an unusual name.

Geoffrey has its origins in Old German and the second half of the name means 'peace'; the first half could come from the words meaning 'god' or 'district'. It was common in the Middle Ages and came back into vogue in the 19th and 20th centuries. The older spelling was Jeffrey but Geoffrey is now the more popular form. Geoff and Jeff are the usual abbreviations.

George comes from the Greek word for 'farmer'. Though St George is the patron saint of England, it was the four Hanoverian King Georges who popularized the name and it remained a favourite for two centuries. It has been out of fashion in Britain in recent years. Georgie is a pet form.

Georgina is the feminine form of George (see above) and was probably more popular in the 1980s than in any other decade. Other versions are Georgiana, Georgia (for example, singer Georgia Brown) and the French form Georgette (for example, writer Georgette Heyer).

Gerald is made up of two Old German words meaning 'spear' and 'rule'. It is an old-established name but went out of use in England for some time. Irish parents continued using the name and it came back into favour in the 19th century. Other spellings are Gerrold, Jerald or Jerold and nicknames are Gerry or Jerry.

Geraldine is the feminine form of Gerald (see above). It was invented by the poet Henry Howard, Earl of Surrey, in the 16th century but was only taken up by parents once Gerald came into fashion. Another spelling is Geraldene. The actress Geraldine McEwan is a well-known bearer of the name. Gerry is also used as a shortened form.

Gerard has similar origins to those of Gerald (see above), two old German words meaning 'spear' and 'brave'. It was so common in the Middle Ages that it produced surnames such as Garrard and Garrett. Another form of the name is Jerrard and the abbreviations are Gerry and Jerry.

Gerry see **Gerald, Gerard** and **Geraldine**

Gertrude comes from the Old German meaning 'spear strength'. The 7th century St Gertrude of Belgium was the patron saint of travellers. Abbreviations include Gertie and Trudy.

Gideon comes from the Hebrew meaning 'one-handed'. It was one of the Biblical names adopted by the Puritans in the 17th century and has been used, though not frequently, ever since.

Gilbert derives from two Old German words and means 'bright pledge'. It is an old-established name which, in medieval times, gave rise to surnames such as Gilbertson, Gilson and Gibbs and it has always been well liked in Scotland and the north of England. Short forms are Gil, Gib and Bert.

Giles is originally from the Greek meaning 'young goat' and was made famous by the 7th century patron saint of beggars and cripples. There are more than 150 churches in Britain dedicated to him. At one time it was a country name, hence 'Farmer Giles', but it now has a better more sophisticated image and is well used by parents in recent years. An alternative spelling is Gyles (for example, writer Gyles Brandreth).

Gillian was originally another form of Juliana, the feminine form of Julian (see page 73), supposed to mean 'downy'. It was common in the Middle Ages, then came back into fashion this century with variations including Jillian and Gillianne. The diminutives Jill and Gill have been used since the 15th century.

Gina was originally the pet form of names like Regina or Georgina but has become a personal name in its own right this century, popularized by the actress Gina Lollobrigida.

Ginger is a pet name for Virginia, but can also be used descriptively to mean red-haired. The best-known bearer of the name is the actress Ginger Rogers.

Ginny see **Virginia**

Giselle comes from German meaning 'a pledge'. It was also made popular by the success of the well-loved and timeless ballet of the same name.

Gladys is a Welsh name meaning 'ruler over territory', which was not used outside Wales until nearly the end of the 19th century. Glad is a pet form.

Glen began as a surname meaning 'from the valley' in Welsh and has appeared as a given name for nearly 200 years. This century it has often been used as Glenn, helped by the fame of band-leader Glenn Miller.

Glenda is a Welsh name which means 'holy good'. It was quite unusual in Britain until the actress Glenda Jackson introduced it to a wider public.

Glenys is from the Welsh word for 'holy' and it has been used quite often in the 1900s with variations including Glenis, Glennis and Glenice. The shortened form is Glen. However, it has diminished in popularity in recent years.

Gloria means 'glory' in Latin and first appeared as a given name at the end of the last century when George Bernard Shaw used it in *You Never Can Tell*. Its popularity was increased by the filmstar Gloria Swanson.

Glyn comes from the Welsh 'valley' and was once exclusive to Wales, though now it is much more widespread.

Glynis, the feminine version of Glyn, comes from the Welsh meaning 'little valley'. In recent years the name has spread beyond Wales, given a boost by the fame of actress Glynis Johns.

Godfrey comes from two Old German words and means 'God's peace'. It came to Britain with the Normans and was common in medieval times. In the past it was often confused with Geoffrey (see page 55) but the two names are now quite distinct. Godfrey is rarely used now.

Golda is derived from the Anglo-Saxon 'gold' and has been in use for 800 years, sometimes in the form Goldie, as in the case of actress Goldie Hawn.

Gordon was originally the name of a famous Scottish family and its meaning is uncertain. It was seldom used as a first name until General Gordon of Khartoum became famous in the late 19th century. Since then it has lost its Scottish associations and is used all over the English-speaking world.

Grace is one of the 'virtue' names favoured by the Puritans and though it faded out for a time it had a new lease of life in Victorian times, after Grace Darling's heroic sea-rescue. Actress Gracie Fields gave its pet form a boost earlier this century, and the late Princess Grace of Monaco, formerly Grace Kelly, kept it in the public eye.

Graham probably stems from the place name Grantham which became the surname of a well-known Scottish family. This century the name has been extremely popular as a personal name with both Scottish and English parents. Other spellings are Grahame and Graeme.

Grant was originally a surname derived from the French word for 'tall'. American parents began using it as a first name in the time of General Grant, President of the USA, 1869-76 and its use spread.

Greg and **Gregg** see **Gregory**

Gregory comes from the Greek and means 'watchful'. Sixteen popes used the name and the pet forms Greg and Grig gave rise to surnames such as Gregg, Grigson and Greig. This century it had a boost through the fame of actor Gregory Peck and has been well used in England and the USA. Scottish parents sometimes use Grigor.

Guinevere, from the Welsh for 'fair and yielding' was the name of King Arthur's queen. The old Cornish version Jenifer gave rise to the modern Jennifer. Guenevere is an alternative spelling, but both are rare.

Guy has uncertain origins, perhaps coming from the Old German meaning 'wood' or 'wide', and was common before the exploits of Guy Fawkes put it out of favour. Parents have taken it up again in recent years.

Gwendoline derives from the Welsh meaning 'white' and with the spelling Gwendolen it is an old-established name in Welsh history. It came into general use in Britain in the last century. Other variations are Gwenda, Gwendolyn and Gwendolene and the abbreviations Gwen and Gwenda are used as independent names.

Gwyn is a boy's name widely used in Wales. It means 'fair'.

Gwyneth is another Welsh name, meaning 'blessed'. It has spread to England but is still more popular with Welsh parents. An alternative spelling is Gwynneth and short forms are Gwyn and Gwinny.

Hamish has evolved from the Gaelic form of James (see page 68) and though well used in Scotland has never caught on in the rest of Britain.

Hammond is derived from the German for 'home' and is properly a surname, used occasionally as a first name, as in the case of the writer Hammond Innes.

Hank is an American form of Henry which is very popular in the USA but unusual in Britain. It is based on the Dutch Henk.

Hannah is from the Hebrew meaning 'God has favoured me' and was the name of the prophet Samuel's mother in the Old Testament. It survived the centuries to become a favourite in Victorian times though the Greek form, Anne (see page 21), has always been more popular. Along with other Victorian names, modern parents have made good use of it. Actress Hannah Gordon has kept it in the public eye.

Harold derives from two Old English words and means 'ruler of the army'. It was at the height of its popularity in the 19th century and ex-Prime Minister Harold Wilson (Lord Wilson) kept it in the public eye in modern times. Variations are Harald and Harrold and it is often shortened to Harry or Hal.

Harriet evolved from Harry, a nickname for Henrietta (see page 62) meaning 'ruler at home'. Another spelling is Harriot and short forms are Harry, Hattie and Hatty. The name was fashionable in the 18th and 19th centuries and has recently come back into favour. A well-known bearer of the name was the greatly admired British actress and comedienne Hattie Jacques.

Harry is a pet form of Henry and an anglicization of Henri, but so well-liked that it is considered as an individual name, particularly since the second son of the Prince and Princess of Wales was given this name.

Harvey originally comes from an Old Breton name meaning 'battle-worthy' and was the name of a 5th century saint. It was common in the Middle Ages, giving rise to surnames such as Harvey, Hervey and Harveson and came back in favour with Victorian parents, though it is still more popular in the USA. It is shortened to Harve and Herve.

Hattie and **Hatty** see **Harriet**

Haydn is from the Celtic meaning 'fire' and is well liked by Welsh parents. Spelling variations are Hayden and Haydon.

Hayley is originally a place name meaning 'hay hill' and has been used as a given name in recent years, following the fame of actress Hayley Mills.

Hazel is one of the tree and flower names which were first taken up as personal names at the end of the last century. Other spellings are Hazell and Hazelle. Singer Hazel O'Connor is a well-known bearer of the name.

Heath was originally used as a surname but has become more popular as a Christian name in recent years.

Heather is another of the botanical names used by late 19th-century parents as first names and was especially successful in the middle years of this century.

Heidi is the pet form of the German name Adelheid, meaning 'nobility'. It spread to other countries with the fame of the 19th century children's book *Heidi* by Johanna Spyri and has been very popular with American and British parents in recent years.

Helen comes from Greek and means 'the bright one'. The name became well known through St Helena, mother of the Emperor

Constantine. It was frequently used from early times in Wales and when it spread to England it was usually in the form of Ellen. Ever since, Ellen and Helen have been changing places as the more popular form of the name: at the moment Helen is the fashionable version. The German shortening of the name Lena is sometimes used and another pet form is Nell.

Henrietta is the feminine version of Henry (see below) meaning 'home ruler', which came to Britain through the French wife of Charles I; her name was Henriette Marie but the British called her Henrietta Maria. The name was at its most popular in the late 19th century and the usual abbreviations are Etta, Etty and Hetty.

Henry is from the Old German meaning 'home-ruler'. Harry, now used as a pet form or an independent name, was the original English version of the name with Henry taking over in the 17th century. England has been ruled by eight King Henrys and among the recent name-bearers have been the statesman Henry Kissinger and the actor Henry Fonda. Nicknames are Hal, Harry and, in America especially, Hank.

Herbert comes from the Old German meaning 'bright army'. It was popular at the turn of the century but has been little used recently. Bert and Bertie are common abbreviations, and, in the USA, Herb and Herbie.

Herman is an Old German name from two words meaning 'army' and 'man'. It is still thought of as a German name though sometimes used in Britain. In the USA it is more widely used.

Hermione comes from Hermes, the name of the messenger of the gods in Greek mythology. It was used as a girl's name by 16th-century writers, notably Shakespeare, but has always been a rather uncommon name.

Hetty see **Esther** and **Henrietta**

Hilary derives from the Greek word for 'cheerful'. It was first used as a boy's name, then in the 12th and 13th centuries it was used for both boys and girls before fading out of use. It came back into favour in the last century and, though still sometimes used for boys, is now mainly a female name.

Hilda has evolved from an Old German term denoting 'battle-maid'. It was made famous by an Anglo-Saxon abbess of Whitby. Always popular in the north while out of favour in the rest of the country, it came back into vogue, with other saints' names, in the late 19th century. A modern spelling is Hylda.

Hildegard is a German name whose meaning is unclear, but the first part means 'battle'. It is occasionally used in Britain and the USA.

Hiram comes from the Hebrew and means 'exalted brother'. It was first used as a name in the 17th century by the Puritans but it has not been widely used in recent years.

Holly is a modern name taken from the name of the plant and often used for girls born around Christmas time. Young parents have made good use of it, though it is more popular in the USA than in Britain. Alternative spellings are Holli and Holley. The name of the heroine of *Breakfast at Tiffany's* is Holly Golightly.

Homer is a Greek name meaning 'pledge'. The great epic poem *The Odyssey* was written by Homer but in spite of its classical associations the name is rarely used in England.

Honey see **Honor**

Honor derives from the Latin for 'honour' or 'reputation', originally used as Honoria, the name of one of the virgins martyred with St Ursula in the 4th century. After the Reformation, when 'virtue' names were popular, it was often spelt Honour. One of the best known modern bearers is actress Honor Blackman. Variations include Honey.

Hope was one of the virtue names which were particularly favoured by 17th century Puritans. In early times the name was used for both boys and girls. It is now used only as a girl's name and has been rarely used in recent years.

Horace and Horatio come from the name of a renowned Roman family, Horatius. Admiral Horatio Nelson was a famous bearer of the name, which is no longer fashionable.

Hortense is the French form of a Latin family name which is occasionally borrowed by English parents for their daughters.

Howard comes from a surname with an aristocratic pedigree as the family name of the Dukes of Norfolk, but its origins are uncertain; it may mean either 'protection' or 'heart'. It has come into general use as a Christian name in the last 100 years or so, unaffected by changes in fashion. The usual abbreviation is Howie.

Hugh is from Old German meaning 'mind' and came to England with the Normans in the Latin form Hugo. It was made popular by the learned 11th-century bishop St Hugh of Lincoln and stayed in fashion for the next 500 years. An alternative spelling is Hew and the Welsh use Huw; pet forms are Huey and Hughie. Other related forms are the Latin version Hugo and Hubert which means 'bright mind'; both are in common use throughout Britain.

Humphrey may be derived from the Old German 'giant peace' or be of Anglo-Saxon origin, the first part meaning 'honey'. The late actor Humphrey Bogart and the musician Humphrey Lyttleton are two modern bearers of the name.

I

Ian is a modern version of John (see page 72) and means 'God is gracious'. It soon spread beyond Scotland to become a favourite all over Britain. Iain is an alternative spelling.

Ianthe comes from the Greek and means 'violet flower'. It was a name favoured by Romantic poets in the 19th century but is not so common today.

Ida is from the Old German 'woman'. It fell into disuse until Tennyson's 19th century poem 'The Princess' brought it to public attention, more so the poem was used as the basis of an operetta by Gilbert and Sullivan. Since then it has gone out of fashion again.

Idris is an old Welsh name meaning 'fiery lord' and is still very common in Wales.

Ila comes from the French 'from the island'. Isla is an alternative spelling more popular today.

Illeana and Ilona are modern variants of Eleanor.

Imogen comes from Shakespeare's *Cymbeline* but was a printer's error for the name Innogen, probably meaning 'girl'. Over the generations it has become an uncommon first name, taken up more often by parents this century. A well-known bearer was the musician Imogen Holst.

Ingrid is derived from the Old Norse name Ing, the god of fertility and has always been popular in Scandinavia. It spread to Europe and America with the fame of the actress Ingrid Bergman. More recently the name in the headlines has been that of the record-breaking runner Ingrid Kristiansen.

Iona comes from the Greek meaning 'violet-coloured stone' but it is now associated with the Hebridean island. The name is very popular in Scotland.

Ira is from the Hebrew and means 'watcher'.

Irene comes from the Greek for 'peace' and has only been used in England for the last 100 years. It was most fashionable in the early part of this century and is still quite popular in Scotland. A variation is Irena and the shortened forms are Rena and Rene.

Iris is from the Greek word for 'rainbow' and became accepted as a personal name at the end of the 19th century when many flower and tree names were in vogue. The best-known modern Iris is the novelist Iris Murdoch.

Irma is of German origin, a short form of Ermintrude, which has spread to English-speaking countries.

Irving and Irwin are from the Anglo-Saxon 'boar-friend' and are examples of a surname being used as a first name. Irving Berlin, the songwriter, was a famous bearer of the name.

Isaac stems from the Hebrew word meaning 'laughter' and appears in the Old Testament as the name of the son of Abraham and Sarah. It was at its most popular with other Biblical names in the 17th century when a famous bearer was scientist Isaac Newton who was famous for his research into gravity. Another spelling is Izaak and diminutives are Ike and Ikey.

Isabel was originally a variation of Elizabeth (see page 46), meaning 'oath of God', which became popular in France before it spread to Britain and became a special favourite in Scotland. Variations are Isabella, Isabelle and Isobel and pet names are Belle, Bella, Isa and Izzy.

Isadora is the feminine form of Isidore, and became known because of the dancer Isadora Duncan who flourished at the beginning of this century.

Isla see **Ila**

Isolde is an ancient Celtic name meaning 'fair one'. Wagner's *Tristan and Isolde* renewed interest in the name.

Ivan is the Russian version of John (see page 72), meaning "God is gracious', which has been adopted by English-speaking parents in modern times and is now quite well known. The seldom-used feminine form is Ivanna.

Ivor is an old-established Celtic name but its meaning is uncertain. It gave rise to Scottish surnames like MacIvor and MacIver. Welsh parents use Ifor, which means 'lord'.

Ivy is one of the plant names favoured in the late 19th century which remained popular for the early part of the 20th.

J

Jacinta comes from the flower name Hyacinth.

Jack began life as a short form of John (see page 72), meaning 'God is gracious', but it became established as an independent name over 100 years ago and was very popular early this century.

Jackie and **Jacky** see **Jacqueline**

Jacob comes from the Hebrew for 'supplanter'; in the Old Testament Jacob tricked his brother Esau out of his inheritance. It came into general use after the Reformation, though now it is mainly used by Jewish families. Today the short form Jake is used as an independent name.

Jacqueline derives from the French version of James or Jacob (see above), meaning 'supplanter' and has been used in England as far back as the 13th century. It has been a top favourite this century and a famous name-bearer is Jacqueline Onassis, formerly the wife of President Kennedy. An old variation of the name is Jacquetta and there are many spellings, including Jacquelyn, Jaqueline and Jacalyn. The usual abbreviation is Jackie or Jacky.

Jacquetta see **Jacqueline**

Jade originates from the Eastern precious stone. It became popular when singer Mick Jagger called his first child Jade.

Jake is a short form of Jacob which is now used independently.

James developed from the name Jacob (see above), meaning 'supplanter'. Though there were two apostles called James, it only became popular once James Stuart became King of England in 1603. One famous bearer is ex-Prime Minister James Callaghan. Pet forms include Jem, Jim, Jimmy and Jamie.

Jamie is one of the abbreviated forms of James which is now used as a name in its own right, both for boys and girls.

Jane is one of the feminine forms of John (see page 72) deriving from the Hebrew meaning 'God is gracious'. It was a very common name for 150 years until the mid-1800s and came back into favour this century. Jayne is an alternative spelling and well-known modern Janes include the actresses Jane Wyman and Jane Fonda and the skater Jayne Torvill. Jinny is sometimes used as a pet form.

Janet was taken by Scottish parents from the French form Jeanette, originally a diminutive of Jane (see page above). Janine, Janette and Janetta all come from the same root. At its most popular in the 19th century, it is now a well-established name and has its own diminutives: Netta, Nettie, Jessie and Jan.

Janice is another diminutive of Jane (see page above) which has only emerged in modern times, adopted by British parents from the USA. Another spelling is Janis.

Jared comes from the Hebrew meaning 'rose' and has been used regularly, though not frequently, as given name for boys since the 17th century. Alternative forms are Jarod and Jareth.

Jasmine is a flower name introduced in the 19th century. The Asian rendering Yasmine which is sometimes used has a softer sound.

Jason is the English form of the Greek name of the writer of the Book of Ecclesiasticus. It was also the name of the hero of the legend of the Golden Fleece. Its meaning is uncertain; possibly 'healer' from the Greek. It first became popular in America and has been one of the top favourites in Britain this century.

Jasper probably comes from the East but its exact origins are unknown. Alternative forms are Casper and Gasper.

Jay comes from the bird name which in English-Old French meant 'chattering'.

Jean comes from the old French form Jehane, yet another name which derives from the Latin feminine of John (see page 72). Robert Burns used the name in his poetry and it became very popular with Scottish parents before it did with the rest of Britain early this century. Other forms include Jeanne and Jeannette.

Jedidiah is a Hebrew name meaning 'friend of Jehovah'. The short form, Jed, is more often used today.

Jefferson is from the surname meaning 'son of Geoffrey' and was first used by American parents Thomas Jefferson, only spreading to Britain in recent years. The short form is Jeff.

Jeffrey see **Geoffrey**

Jem see **James**

Jemima derives from the Hebrew for 'dove' and appears in the Old Testament as the name of one of the daughters of Job. It was adopted by the Puritans and became a common name in the 1800s. Pet names are Jem, Jemmy and Mima.

Jennifer began as a Cornish version of the name Guenevere, meaning 'fair lady', and only spread throughout the country in modern times. Jenny is the short form.

Jeremy has the grand meaning 'God exalts', stemming from the Hebrew and in modern times has taken over in popularity from the more formal Jeremiah. Both are shortened to Jerry, which is also used as an independent name.

Jerrard see **Gerard**

Jerry see **Jeremy** and **Jerome**

Jerome is from ancient Greek meaning 'holy name'. The song writer Jerome Kern has made the name familiar. Jerry is a shortened form.

Jesse comes from the Hebrew meaning 'the Lord exists' and, in the Old Testament, is the name of King David's father. It was first used by parents after the Reformation and has survived the generations. It was publicized earlier this century by the athlete Jesse Owens.

Jessica meaning 'he beholds', is from the Hebrew, and for many generations was only used in Jewish families. Shakespeare's use of it in *The Merchant of Venice* brought it into general usage and it has been gaining in popularity in recent years. The diminutive Jessie is used as a name in its own right.

Jessie see **Janet** and **Jessica**

Jill is a short form of Gillian which has been very successful in its own right.

Jinny see **Jane** and **Virginia**

Joan is one of the feminine forms of John, like Jane and Jean (see pages 69 and 70), and meaning 'God is gracious'. It was such a common name in Shakespeare's time that it faded out of fashion through over-use but it was again a top favourite in the early 1900s. Famous modern Joans include the actresses Joan Crawford and Joan Collins.

Joanne and Joanna are both short forms of the earlier spelling Johanna and are further feminine versions of John, 'God is gracious'. They have both been popular in recent years, given a boost by the fame of actress Joanna Lumley.

Jocelyn is an ancient German name, probably originally meaning 'a Goth' and was commonly used in Britain in the Middle Ages, though always as a boy's name. It has been used for girls only in modern times and spellings include Jocelin, Joscelin and Josslyn. Cookery writer Josceline Dimbleby is a female bearer of the name and actor Joss Ackland a male Jocelyn.

Jodie is a variation of Judy, the shortened form of Judith, and is gaining popularity in its own right.

Joel comes from the Hebrew 'Jehovah is the Lord' and was the name of one of the minor prophets of the Old Testament. The Normans brought it to Britain as a personal name.

John means 'God is gracious' from the Hebrew. It is an important Biblical name, belonging to St John the Baptist and St John the beloved disciple and has been popular with parents since the Middle Ages. Pet forms are Johnny, Johnnie and Jack (see page 68), which is also an independent name. The best-known modern John was probably the US President John F. Kennedy. Jon is an alternative spelling.

Jolie is thought to be derived from Julia, though in recent times it has become a name in its own right.

Jonas, from the Hebrew word for 'dove', is the favoured form of Jonah, the name of the Old Testament prophet which became associated with bad luck. It has survived the generations without ever being particularly popular.

Jonathan derives from the Hebrew and means 'gift of God'. In the Old Testament it is the name of King David's close friend. It has been widely used in England only since the Reformation and is quite popular today. Other spellings are Jonathon and Jonothon and short forms are Jon or Jonnie.

Joseph means 'may the Lord add' in Hebrew and is the New Testament name for the husband of the Virgin Mary and Joseph of Arimathea. At first it was used mainly by Jewish families but by the 19th century it was widespread and it has been a favourite in Britain and the USA in recent times. It is often shortened to Jo, Joe, Josie or Joey.

Josephine is the French feminine diminutive of Joseph (see above), meaning 'may the Lord add' and was made popular by Napoleon's Empress Joséphine. Short forms are Jo and Josie, which is often used as an independent name.

Joshua comes from the Hebrew meaning 'God saves' and is another form of the name Jesus. It has become popular in English-speaking countries in the past few years and is abbreviated to Josh.

Josie see **Joseph** and **Josephine**

Joy is a simple name which means just what it says and dates back to the 12th century. After a period of neglect it came back into favour in the first half of this century.

Joyce is from the name of a 7th century Breton saint which may originally have come from the Old German for 'a Goth'. In the Middle Ages it was a common name, given to both boys and girls, but when it swung back into fashion in the 1900s it was mostly used for girls.

Judith is a very old name meaning 'a Jewess' in Hebrew but it is only since the 17th century that the name has been widely used. The pet form Judy or Judi is often used in its own right, for example, the actress Dame Judi Dench, and a modern variation is Jody or Jodie.

Julia and its variation Juliana are feminine versions of the Latin name Julius, meaning 'downy' or 'hairy'. It was much used by parents in the 18th century, but in modern times has been overtaken by the French form Julie. Today's well-known bearers include the actresses Julie Andrews, Julie Christie and Julia Foster.

Julian comes originally from the Latin name Julius which meant 'downy' or 'hairy' and is the name of many saints, but it has only been used widely by parents this century. The variation Jolyon, used primarily in the north of England, became widely known through John Galsworthy's *The Forsyte Saga*.

Juliet comes from the Italian Giulietta, a diminutive of Giulia from which we may take our Julia (but see also 'Julian'). Its popularity is due to the use Shakespeare made of it in the great tragic love story *Romeo and Juliet*. Nowadays the name is sometimes spelt Juliette and a bearer is popular singer Juliette Greco.

June is the name of the month used as a girl's name over the past 60 years, along with April (see page 22). It has been kept before the public eye by actress June Whitfield.

Justin derives from the Latin for 'just' and is an old-established name which was used by Irish parents before it shot into fashion all over the English-speaking world in the past decade.

Justine is the French feminine form of Justin (see above), meaning 'just', which is now more popular than the long-established Justina, the name of a 4th-century martyr.

Kane is an unusual boy's name which comes from the Welsh 'beautiful' or Manx 'warrior'.

Karen is the Danish form of Catherine (see page 32) meaning 'pure', and came to Britain from the USA. It has been a modern favourite in both countries with all sorts of variations, including Kara, Karena, Karin and Karon. Most of the forms also appear with a 'C' spelling.

Karl see **Charles** and **Carl**

Kate is a short form of Katharine which was popular in Shakespeare's day and in Victorian times. It is now an accepted name in its own right. Katy or Katie is the pet form.

Katharine or Katherine is simply an alternative spelling for Catherine, but is the form which has given rise to variations such as Kate, Kathy or Kitty.

Kathleen is the Irish form of Katharine and is widely used. Cathleen is an alternative but less popular spelling.

Kathy see **Katherine**

Kay was originally a nickname for any girl whose name began with a 'K', as well as a diminutive of Karen and Katherine, but it has recently established itself as an independent name, often spelled as Kaye.

Kegan is an unusual boy's name which is the Irish equivalent of Hugh, and has been said to mean 'little fiery one'.

Keith comes originally from a Scottish place name which may mean 'wind' or 'wood'. It was taken up as a family name and spread to England as a first name at the turn of the century, becoming widely used. A well-known bearer is politician Sir Keith Joseph.

Kelly is a modern personal name taken from a Gaelic surname meaning 'warrior' and has been a great favourite over the past few years.

Kelvin was originally the name of a Scottish river, possibly meaning 'narrow stream', used as a given name since the middle of this century. Another spelling is Kelvyn.

Kenneth comes from the old Gaelic word meaning 'handsome'. It was popular with Scottish parents from the time of Kenneth MacAlpine, the first king of Scotland. Over the past 100 years it has been used widely, making its biggest impact in Britain in the 1920s and has lost its strong Scottish associations. Short forms are Ken and Kenny.

Kent comes from the name of the south-eastern county, which may originally have meant 'corner land'. Together with the variation Kenton it became a surname which was recently taken up by parents, both in Britain and other English-speaking countries, as a boy's first name.

Kerry comes from the Irish county name, originally meaning 'dark'. Over the past few years it has been used by parents in increasing numbers as a given name. Other spellings are Kerri and Kerrie.

Kevin is a Gaelic name meaning 'comely at birth' and made popular by St Kevin, the 10th century abbot of Glendalough in County Wicklow, so that it was common among Irish families long before it spread more widely in the 1900s and became a favourite with British and American parents.

Kieran is from the Celtic for 'dark' and though two 6th century Irish saints bore the name it was only rediscovered this century, first in Ireland, then in Scotland and later by English parents, coming into vogue over the past decade. Other commonly used variants are Kieron and Kieren.

Kim is a popular girl's name that began as a short form of Kimberley (see below). The boy's version is a short form of Kimball, an Anglo-Saxon name for 'kinbold', and it was used by Rudyard Kipling for the hero of his novel *Kim*.

Kimball see **Kim**

Kimberley was originally a surname taken from the place name meaning 'Cyneburg's wood' or 'clearing'. As a personal name it suddenly shot into fashion in the USA 20 or 30 years ago and spread to Britain. It is sometimes used for boys but far more often for girls and a frequent spelling is Kimberly, with variations including Kimberlee and Kimber.

Kirk is taken from the surname meaning 'church' and has been used as a Christian name for over 100 years. It was re-popularized in modern times by the fame of the actor Kirk Douglas, though it is used more in the USA than in Britain.

Kirsty has long been the Scottish form of Christine (see page 34) and has now come into vogue with families all over the country. Variations include Kirstie, Kirstyn and Kirsteen.

Kit is a short form of Christopher and sometimes used as an individual name. Kitty is not the feminine version, but an abbreviation formed from Katharine.

Kurt is the diminutive of the German name Konrad, meaning 'bold counsel', used in Britain in recent years as a name in its own right, sometimes spelt Curt.

Kyle is a Gaelic name used for both boys and girls, and means 'handsome'.

Kylie is a girl's name meaning 'boomerang' and has long been popular in Australia. Singer Kylie Minogue has made the name more widely known. It is sometimes spelt Kyly.

Lana is from the Greek for 'shining' and is occasionally used in the USA. The Irish Alana, 'my child' is a similar name more likely to be used in Britain.

Lance is derived from the Old German word meaning 'land' and is the short form of Lancelot, a name made famous through the hero from the Arthurian legends. Lancelot was used by 19th century parents but has now almost disappeared. Lance, which first appeared in Victorian times, has been popular this century.

Lara probably originates from the Latin for 'famous' and, as a first name, it caught the imagination of English-speaking parents following the spectacular 1960s film of Boris Pasternak's *Doctor Zhivago* with its haunting theme music, 'Lara's theme'. An alternative spelling is Larah.

Laura has obscure origins but may be from the Latin meaning 'laurel'. It is an old-established name, in the past especially favoured by Welsh parents but now very fashionable all over Britain. Other versions are the older form Lora, the French forms Laurette and Lorette and, particularly in the USA, Laurel, Lauren, Laureen and Lauri.

Laureen see **Laura**

Laurel see **Laura**

Lauren see **Laura**

Laurence derives from the Latin name given to a man from Laurentium, the 'city of laurels.' It was made famous by the 3rd century martyr St Laurence and has given rise to surnames like Lowrie, Larkins and Lawson. In modern times it is often used as Lawrence and had a boost from the fame of Lawrence of Arabia. Short forms are Laurie and Larry (for example, actor Larry Hagman).

Lavinia is a classical name that was popular during the Renaissance. It faded out of fashion in the 19th century but is still used occasionally. Vinnie is a short form.

Leanna is thought to come from the French *Liane* which means 'climbing vine'. Other versions include Leanne, Liana and Leana.

Lee was originally a surname from the Anglo-Saxon for 'meadow'. It was first used as a personal name by American parents, and has become popular in Britain. It is usually a boy's name but can also be used for girls (e.g. actor Lee Marvin and actress Lee Remick) and the alternative form is Leigh.

Leila finds its roots in a Persian name meaning 'dark-haired', used by Lord Byron in hs works in the early 19th century and taken up by parents later. Variations are Leilah, Lela and Lila.

Len and **Lennie** see **Leonard**

Lena is a German shortened form of Helena, but also recognized as an independent name, for example the American singer and actress Lena Horne.

Leo comes from the Latin for 'lion' and 13 popes have taken the name so it has always been favoured by Roman Catholic parents, while Jewish families prefer the form Leon. Well-known modern bearers are the singer Leo Sayer and politician Leon Brittan. Variations used for girls are Leona and Leonie.

Leonard is made up from two Old German words meaning 'lion' and 'brave' and has been in fairly regular use since the Middle Ages, with a successful spell in the early 1900s. Pet names are Len and Lenny. The late actor Leonard Rossiter has publicized the name in recent years.

Leonora is a name which occurs in many languages and may be a derivation of the name Eleanor (see page 46). It was made popular in England in the 19th century as the name of the heroine in Beethoven's opera *Fidelio*.

Leroy comes from the Old French meaning 'the king'. Until recent times it was regarded as an American name but it is now frequently used in Britain by families of West Indian origin.

Leslie was originally a Scottish place name, probably meaning 'little meadow', taken up as a surname. It has been used as a first name for both boys and girls since the 18th century and though the usual masculine form is Leslie and the feminine Lesley, the spellings are interchangeable. As a boy's name it was at its peak in the early 1900s, with the girl's form becoming popular later.

Lester is taken from the surname originally given to someone who came from Leicester, and though an uncommon first name it has been kept in the public eye by jockey Lester Piggott.

Letitia comes from Latin and means 'full of joy and happiness'. Lettice is a variant and used to be common in Tudor England.

Lewis is the anglicized version of the name Louis (see page 82), meaning 'famous in war'. Welsh parents have used it regularly as an alternative for Llewellyn and it was brought to public attention in England by Lewis Carroll, author of *Alice in Wonderland*. The abbreviation is Lew.

Liam is an Irish version of William (see page 121), meaning 'helmet', which has been taken up by non-Irish parents.

Libby is a pet form of Elizabeth which is occasionally used as a name in its own right.

Lilian has uncertain origins; it may have developed from a pet form of Elizabeth (see page 46) or from the name of the flowering lily. It made its biggest impact around the turn of the century and is often shortened to Lil or Lily. Variations are Lillie, Lilia and Lilian and Scottish parents sometimes use Lilias.

Lily is a personal name in its own right as well as a short form of Lilian, and became popular with the Victorian vogue for flower names. The actress Lily Tomlin is a modern bearer of the name.

Linda comes from the old German word meaning 'serpent' and has only been used in Britain over the past 100 years, quickly becoming very popular with parents all over the English-speaking world, though it is now out of fashion again. The alternative spelling is Lynda and the short forms Lin, Lyn, Lynn, Lynne and Lindy are used as names in their own right.

Lindsay derives from a place name in Lincolnshire and was first used as a given name by Scottish parents, first for boys, then for both boys and girls. It is widely popular in the present generation as a girl's name with spellings including Lindsey and Lynsey.

Linnet or Lynette is a version of the Welsh Eiluned, meaning 'icon', but also the name of a songbird. The 19th century poet Tennyson used Lynette in *Idylls of the King*, and this is the preferred spelling.

Lionel comes from the French meaning 'little lion'. Edward III called his son Lionel and parents have used it steadily ever since. It went through a popular phase early this century. Television personality Lionel Blair is a modern bearer of the name.

Lisa see **Elizabeth**

Lise and **Lisette** see **Elizabeth**

Liza see **Elizabeth**

Llewellyn, also written Llywelyn, is a Celtic name meaning 'like a lion' and is an old-established favourite in Wales, though it has been used far less often in recent years. It is abbreviated to Llew or Lyn.

Lloyd traces its descent from the Welsh word for 'grey' and is a common surname and popular as a first name, having spread to families without Welsh connections earlier this century through the popularity of Prime Minister Lloyd George.

Lois is a girl's name whose meaning is unclear, though it is known to be Greek. It was first used in England in the 17th century.

Loretta is a well-used Roman Catholic name, possibly deriving from Our Lady of Loreto in Italy. Country singer Loretta Lyn is a modern bearer of the name. Another version is Lauretta, and both forms may derive from Laura (see page 78).

Lorna may be derived from an old English word meaning 'forsaken' and was invented by R.D. Blackmore for his novel *Lorna Doone* in 1869. It has been used, especially in Scotland, ever since. Variations are Lorena and Lorne, which is used for boys.

Lorraine comes from a French place name and was first used as a given name by Scottish parents. In the middle of this century it was a favourite in both Britain and the USA, with its alternative spellings Loraine and Lorayne.

Lottie and **Lotty** see **Charlotte**

Louella is a combination of Louise and Ella

Louis, made up from two Old German words meaning 'famous in war', was a favourite name for generations of French kings. English parents first used the form Lewis (see page 80), though Louis has been favoured in Scotland pronounced in the French way, for example, the writer Robert Louis Stevenson. Pet names are Lou and Louie.

Louise is the feminine form of Louis (see above) and means 'famous in war'. In the 19th century the form Louisa was much in vogue but Louise has replaced it as a recent favourite. Abbreviations are Lou and Lulu.

Lucas see **Luke**

Lucille see **Lucy**

Lucinda is a poetic version of Lucy fashionable in the 17th century. Cindy is the short form.

Lucy derives from the Latin word for 'light' and in early times was given to children born at daybreak. It was a top favourite in Victorian times and is now back in fashion again. Other forms are Lucia, Lucie and Lucille.

Luke and the earlier form Lucas derive from the Greek name meaning 'man of Luciana' and was popularized by the writer of the third gospel. It came to Britain with the Normans and gave rise to names such as Lucas, Luck and Lukin. Though it has never been a favourite with British parents, it has become more popular over the past few years.

Luther comes from the Old German word for 'famous army' and is associated with the 16th century religious reformer Martin Luther. It is still used in the USA where the late Martin Luther King made it famous.

Lydia comes from the Greek meaning 'woman of Lydia' and though it appears in the Bible, it only became widely used in the middle of the 18th century and has survived ever since. The pet name is Liddy.

Lyle is an unusual boy's name derived from old French meaning 'island'.

Lyn, Lynn and **Lynne** see **Linda**

Mabel is believed to have derived from the Old English name Amabel, but may come from the French *ma belle*, meaning 'my beautiful girl'.

Madeleine, the French version of the name Magdalene, meaning 'woman of Magdala', was used for St Mary Magdalene in the Bible. It has been popular with parents this century and has many varying forms including Madeline, Madaleine and Madilyn.

Madge see **Margaret**

Mae see **Margaret**

Maeve was a legendary Irish warrior queen.

Magnus comes from the Latin meaning 'great', and it has been widely used in Scandinavia, the Shetland Islands, Scotland and Ireland, where Manus is the usual form. The T.V. personality Magnus Magnusson has recently brought it into the public eye.

Maisie is a Scottish short form of Margaret, used as a name in its own right, as in the story *What Maisie Knew* by Henry James.

Malcolm comes from the Gaelic meaning 'servant of St Columba'. It has been a favourite in Scotland, with four Scottish kings bearing the name and in modern times has been in widespread use. Conductor Sir Malcolm Sargent has kept the name in the public eye.

Mamie is an American pet form of Mary, also given as Mame.

Mandy is a modern short form of Amanda or Miranda, which is now recognized as an individual name.

Marcia is a feminine version of Mark (see page 86), meaning 'war-like', which has been used over the past 100 years. American parents have used it more, often spelling it Marsha. Variations are Marcella and Marcelle and pet names are Marcy and Marcie.

Marcus see **Mark**

Margaret stems from a Greek word meaning 'pearl'. It was one of the most successful girl's names for well over 300 years and though it is not in vogue today it is stil frequently used by Scottish parents. It has numerous variations including Margot, Margaretta and Marguerite and short forms including Madge, Mae, Meg, Meggie, Maggie, Peg and Peggy. Prime Minister Margaret Thatcher is one of the best-known modern Margarets.

Margery was originally a form of Margaret (see above), evolving from the French version Marguerite but has been an independent name since early times. At first Margery was the English and Marjorie the Scottish form but they are now interchangeable. Abbreviations are Marge and Margie.

Margot see **Margaret**

Maria see **Mary**

Marie is the French form of Mary (see page 86) and, in the present generation, has taken over from Mary as the popular form. Its pet form is Mimi. Marcia is the Italian and Spanish form of Mary.

Marianne see **Marion**

Marilyn comes from a modern combination of the names of Mary and Lynn, popular with American parents. It received a great boost from the fame of the actress Marilyn Monroe to become a favourite around 1950 in both Britain and the USA. Spellings include Mary-lyn, Maralyn and Marrilynne.

Marion is a development from Mary, via the French form Marie (see page 85), often used in medieval times and given a boost by the Robin Hood legends with their heroine Maid Marian. Together with the variants Marian and Marianne it has been frequently used by parents over the past 100 years. It can also be used as a double name, i.e. Mary Ann.

Mark derives from the name of the Roman god of war, Mars and means 'war-like'. It was the name of the author of one of the Gospels but it is only in the past 30 years that it has become one of the most popular boys' names in the English-speaking world. Marcus is still favoured by Jewish families and Marc and Marcel are the French versions. One of the best-known bearers was author Mark Twain.

Marlene is a contraction of Mary Magdalene, for which Marlena was an abbreviation in parts of Europe in the 19th century, and both names are still used. The German singer Marlene Dietrich is a well-known bearer of the name.

Marsha see **Marcia**

Marshall comes from the French-German for 'farrier', and is a surname which has become popular as a first name in the USA.

Martha is a Biblical name from the Aramaic for 'lady'. Though it has never been very fashionable, it has always been in use, and the abbreviations Marty and Marti are well known (for example singer Marti Webb and entertainer Marti Caine).

Martin comes, like Mark (see above) from Mars, the god of war. It was a common name in the Middle Ages, giving rise to surnames such as Martin, Martinson and Martel and has survived through the centuries to be a popular choice until quite recently. The Welsh version is Martyn and feminine forms are Martine and Martina. The usual abbreviation is Marty.

Marvin see **Mervyn**

Mary is such an ancient name that its meaning is lost in time, though there are many guesses: 'wished for child', 'rebellion' and 'bitterness'. It is revered as the name of the Virgin Mary, famous as a royal name and was a top favourite with parents for 300 years, only going out of fashion recently. Among the variations are the Latin form Maria and the Irish Maire and nicknames include Molly, Polly and Minnie.

Matilda and Maud come from two old German words meaning 'strength' and 'battle'. Neither version is common in modern times, though the short forms Tilly, Mattie and Maudie still occur.

Matthew comes from Hebrew meaning 'gift of God' and was so common in the Middle Ages that it produced surnames such as Macey, Matthews and Mayhew. It came back into fashion with the present generation to become one of the most popular boys' names in the English-speaking world. A variation is the older form Matthias and short forms are Mat and Matty.

Maud see **Matilda**

Maureen is a modern name, stemming from a diminutive of the Irish Maire, a form of Mary (see above), which soon spread to the rest of Britain. Actresses Maureen O'Hara and Maureen Lipman have helped to keep it popular. Another spelling is Maurine and the short form is Mo.

Maurice comes from the Latin for 'a Moor'. It was most frequently used by British parents in the first half of this century, often as Morris. French singer Maurice Chevalier was a popular bearer of the name. The pet form Moss is sometimes used as a name in its own right.

Mavis is an old country name for a song thrush and was used as a given name in late Victorian times, when 'nature' names were in vogue.

Max see **Maximilian**

Maxim see **Maximilian**

Maximilian, with its short form, Max, comes from the Latin title of honour meaning 'greatest' and was a favourite name in Germany before spreading to Britain. Maxim and Maxwell are modern, commonly used variations.

Maxine is a modern name stemming from the diminutive of Maximilian and has enjoyed a spell of popularity over the past 20 years. Other spellings are Maxime and Maxeen.

May is a pet form of Mary as well as being the name of a month. Mae is an alternative modern spelling.

Megan is a Welsh name developed from Meg, one of the pet names of Margaret (see page 85) meaning 'pearl'. Its use spread in the early 1900s. Short forms are Meg and Meggy.

Melanie derives from the Greek meaning 'dark-complexioned' and came to Britain with the French Huguenots in the 17th century, when it was used mainly in the West Country. It shot into fashion over 40 years ago when it was used for one of the heroines of the book and film *Gone With the Wind*. Another spelling is Melany and pet forms are Mel and Melly.

Melinda is a combination of Greek and Latin words meaning 'sweet' and 'soft' which was popular in the 17th century.

Melissa is from the Greek word meaning 'a bee'. It was used as a personal name 200 years ago, then made a comeback in the middle of the present century, becoming a top favourite with American parents and also reviving in Britain.

Melody was first used as a girl's name in the late 18th century and means just what it says.

Melvyn has obscure origins; it may be from the Celtic for 'chief' or from the Gaelic meaning 'smooth brow'. It has been used for about 100 years and has been in the public eye recently through writer and broadcaster Melvyn Bragg. It is also used as Melvin and shortened to Mel.

Meredith derives from two Old Welsh words meaning 'great chief'. It was a surname adapted as a boy's given name by Welsh parents in the last century but in recent years, as it spread to other countries, it has been used often for girls. The short form, Merry, is also used as an independent name.

Meriel is a Celtic name and means 'bright as the sea'.

Merle comes from the French for 'blackbird'. Meryl and Merel are variations more commonly used now, and the actress Meryl Streep has given the name a fillip in recent years. Merrill and Merryl are the male variations.

Merlin means 'sea hill' in Old Welsh and was the name of King Arthur's magician. The name is uncommon today.

Merril, Merryl and **Meryl** see **Merle**

Mervyn is from the same Old Welsh word as Merlin meaning 'sea hill'. Alternative versions are Mervin and Marvin. The short form is Merv.

Mia is from the Italian word for 'mine' and its use has grown over the past 20 years, boosted by the fame of the actress Mia Farrow.

Michael derives from the Hebrew meaning 'who is like god.' It has always been a favourite name – so common in Ireland that 'Mick' has become a nickname for any Irishman – and has been one of the most fashionable names this century. Pet forms are Mick, Mickey and Mike and among the famous name-bearers are the actor Michael Caine, composer Sir Michael Tippett and Walt Disney's cartoon character Mickey Mouse. The feminine version Michaela is occasionally used.

Michelle is the French feminine form of Michael (see above). Actress Michelle Dotrice is a well-known bearer. The alternative spelling is Michele.

Mike see **Michael**

Mildred is derived from the Anglo-Saxon meaning 'gentle power' and was favoured by the Victorian. The short form is Milly or Millie.

Miles has uncertain origins but may mean 'beloved'. It is an old-established name brought to England by the Normans and has been used fairly steadily through the years. Other versions are Myles and Milo.

Millicent comes from the Old German meaning 'work' or 'strong' and came to England in the 12th century, in the French form Mélisande. It was fashionable in Victorian times but rather unusual now. Milly and Millie are short forms.

Milo see **Miles**

Milton is an Anglo-Saxon name for 'mill enclosure' and is a surname used occasionally as a first name (for example journalist Milton Shulman).

Mina and **Minna** see **Wilhemina**

Minnie is usually taken to be a Scottish pet form of Mary, but is also an abbreviation from Wilhelmina, the feminine version of William.

Miranda means 'worthy to be admired' in Latin and was coined by Shakespeare for his heroine in *The Tempest*. Parents have taken it up increasingly often in recent years. It shares its short form Mandy with Amanda.

Miriam is the earliest form of Mary (see page 86) and its meaning is uncertain. It is the name of an Old Testament prophetess but only came into use in Britain in the 17th century and is favoured by Jewish families. A well-known modern bearer is writer and broad-caster Dr Miriam Stoppard.

Moira is the phonetic form of the Irish name Maire, from Mary (see page 86), which has been taken up by parents, particularly in Scotland, as an independent name. Singer Moira Anderson has kept it before the public in recent times. Another spelling is Moyra.

Molly is an affectionate form of Mary, which has long been recognized as a name in its own right.

Monica is the name of a 4th century saint, the mother of St Augustine, who came from North Africa. The origins and meaning of the name are unknown. It was often used earlier this century but in the past few years parents have preferred the French form Monique.

Montague comes originally from a French place name meaning 'pointed hill' and came to Britain as a surname with the Norman invasion. Parents first used it at christenings in the 1800s when aristocratic-sounding names were in vogue. Short forms are Monty and Monte.

Morna is an unusual girl's name which comes from the Gaelic for 'beloved'. Myrna is a well known variant.

Morris see **Maurice**

Muriel is an old Celtic name meaning 'sea'. It was popular in the Middle Ages, then fell out of use before coming back into fashion in Victorian times. Meriel is an alternative form.

Murray or Moray is a Celtic clan name, possibly taken from the Moray Firth, which is sometimes taken as a personal name.

Myra is a name invented by the 16th century poet Fulke Greville and was more popular with writers than parents until recent times, when Scottish parents in particular have shown a liking for it.

Myrna see **Morna**

Myron, a boy's name dates back to the days of ancient Greece and means 'fragrant'.

Myrtle comes from the plant of the same name.

Nadia and Nadine both come from the Russian word meaning 'hope' and have been used regularly by English-speaking families this century. Variations include Nada, Nadya and Nadeem. A well-known bearer is the gymnast Nadia Comineci.

Nan see **Ann**

Nancy comes originally from Nan, the pet form for Anne (see page 21) so it has the same meaning, 'grace'. It has been used regularly as a name in its own right for around 200 years.

Naomi means 'pleasant' in Hebrew and is the name of Ruth's mother-in-law in the Old Testament. It was one of the Biblical names favoured by the Puritans and has been in use ever since, though never popular.

Narelle is a charming girls name, originally from Australia.

Natalie comes from the Latin meaning 'the Lord's birthday', and is one of the traditional names for girls born at Christmas. Its popularity over the past 20 years has been helped by the popularity of Russian-born ballerina Natalia Makarova, and it is now a top favourite with British parents. Another version is Nathalie.

Natasha is the Russian pet form of Natalie, which has long been used as an independent name in English-speaking countries. It is sometimes shortened to Tasha.

Nathan stems from the Hebrew word meaning 'a gift' and was the name of an Old Testament prophet. It has been used steadily since the Reformation, mainly by Jewish families, then over the past decade it has become generally popular. Nat and Natty are the usual abbreviations.

Nathaniel means 'God has given' in Hebrew and was one of the Biblical names to come into use after the Reformation, though it has never been a favourite. Short forms are Nat and Nath.

Neda is possible Slavonic and means 'Sunday's child'.

Neil probably comes from the Old Irish for 'champion' and was popular in Scotland long before it was taken up all over Britain, where it has been in fashion for the past 30 years. Other frequent spellings are Neill and Neal. Niall is used in Ireland and Scotland. Among famous modern Neils are the astronaut Neil Armstrong, the singer Neil Sedaka and the politician Neil Kinnock.

Nell is an old form of Eleanor and Helen which has also been used as an independent name, most famously by Charles II's mistress, Nell Gwynne.

Nelson began as a surname meaning 'Nell's son' and came into fashion as a personal name in honour of the hero of Trafalgar, Lord Nelson. It has been kept in the public eye by singer Nelson Eddy and the character Nelson Gabriel in the radio serial *The Archers*.

Nessie see **Nesta**

Nesta is a Welsh name, a pet form of Agnes, and was the name of a 16th century princess. Nessie and Nessa are English versions.

Neville comes originally from a French place name meaning 'new town' and was the surname of a powerful medieval family. It became a personal name in the 17th century.

Niall see **Neil**

Nicholas derives from two Greek words meaning 'victory' and 'people'. It was common in the Middle Ages and has survived the centuries to become popular in many English-speaking countries in recent years. Pet names are Nick, Nicky and sometimes Nico.

Nicola is the feminine form of Nicholas (see page 93) though it has been far more popular than the boy's name, becoming one of the most fashionable names for girls over the past few years. Variations are Nichola and Nicole and the pet form is Nikki. Nicolette is the French diminutive form.

Nigel comes from the same root as Neil meaning 'champion', and has been popular with British parents in recent times. Columnist Nigel Dempster and actors Nigel Havers and Nigel Hawthorne have kept the name in the public eye.

Nina began as a pet form for the Russian Annina or the French Nanine, both versions of Anne (see page 21), meaning 'grace'. It has been used as an independent name over the past 100 years or so, with the variation Ninette.

Ninian is an unusual boy's name, possibly of Celtic origin. The 5th century saint of that name was a bishop of Galway who built a beautiful church of white stone.

Noah is from the Hebrew for 'long lived' or possibly 'repose', and as one of the oldest Biblical names has been in use for centuries, though it is uncommon today.

Noel comes from the French for 'Christmas' and since the Middle Ages has been used as a name for both boys and girls born at this time of year. Nowadays the feminine form is often Noelle. Well-known bearers have been playwright Noël Coward, actress Noele Gordon and TV personality Noel Edmonds.

Nora was originally an Irish diminutive of the name Honora, meaning 'honour' and, with variations Norah and Noreen, it was popular with Irish parents long before it found favour with the English at the turn of the century. Well-known bearers include novelist Norah Lofts and Baroness Norah Phillips.

Noreen see **Nora**

Norma has uncertain origins but may be from the Latin meaning 'rule'. It first appeared as a forename in the title of Bellini's opera *Norma* in 1831, and was popular in England and the USA earlier this century. Parents sometimes use it as a feminine form of Norman (see below).

Norman comes from the Old English name for a 'man from the north' and appears in the Domesday Book. It survived the generations in Scotland and became established once more in the rest of Britain this century. It is often shortened to Norm. A well-known bearer of the name is the politician Norman Tebbit.

Nyree is a Maori word of unknown meaning. It was introduced to Britain by actress Nyree Dawn Porter.

O P Q

Octavia is from Latin and means 'eighth girl'. It is normally used independent of its meaning.

Odette is the French feminine of an Old German name meaning 'rich', used as a given name in Britain this century and made famous by the 1950 film *Odette*, based on the true story of a wartime resistance heroine, though it is still an uncommon name in Britain.

Olga, a Russian name which originally comes from Old Norse, means 'holy'. It became popular in Britain in Victorian times, along with other names adopted from Russia.

Olive see **Olivia**

Oliver has uncertain origins but may stem from a Teutonic name meaning 'elf-host'. It is an old-established name which went out of favour with the fall of Oliver Cromwell, only returning to regular use this century, helped in popularity by comedian Oliver Hardy and actor Oliver Reed. The usual short form is Olly.

Olivia comes from the Latin meaning 'olive'. Olive was used in the Victorian era but modern parents prefer Olivia. Singer Olivia Newton-John has helped to publicize the name.

Olwen comes from the Welsh for 'white footprint'. In ancient legend, Olwen got her name because white clover sprang up wherever her foot touched the ground. It is still used mainly by Welsh parents, often as Olwyn.

Olympia is an ancient Greek name meaning 'heavenly one'. Now-adays its immediate connection is with the Olympic Games.

Orson comes from the Latin word for 'bear'. The English equivalent of the Italian Orso, it is well known because of the fame of Orson Welles, actor and film-maker.

Orville is a French place name meaning 'gold town'. It is best known as the name of the pioneer aviator, Orville Wright.

Oscar comes from the Old English words for 'god' and 'spear'. After Napoleon's godson of that name became king of Sweden the name spread through Europe. Oscar Wilde is still probably the most famous bearer of the name.

Otis is a name used for both girls and boys in the USA, notably the singer Otis Redding. It comes either from the Greek 'keen-eared' or the Old German 'wealthy'.

Owen derives from Latin and means 'well born'. It is a great name in Welsh history and legend and has survived through the ages, being used throughout the English-speaking world but still a special favourite with Welsh parents.

Paddy see **Patricia** and **Patrick**

Paloma comes from Spain and means 'dove'. It has been introduced into Britain by the fame of the designer and celebrity Paloma Picasso.

Pamela stems from two Greek words meaning 'all honey' and was first used as a Christian name in the works of Sir Philip Sidney in the 16th century. It was at its most fashionable around the middle of this century and is often shortened to Pam or Pammie.

Pascal is derived from the French name for Easter. The feminine equivalent is Pascale.

Patience is a virtue name which was introduced in the 17th century and has remained in use, sometimes abbreviated to Pat.

Patricia is the feminine form of Patrick (see below), meaning 'nobleman'. It became popular at the turn of the century through

Queen Victoria's granddaughter, Princess Patricia of Connaught. Short forms are Pat, Patty, Patsy, Paddy, Tricia and Trisha.

Patrick comes from the Latin word for 'nobleman' and was made famous by the 5th century patron saint of Ireland. It has always been so popular there that 'Paddy' has become a nickname for an Irishman but the name is also widely used in Britain and the USA. Pet names are Pat and Paddy.

Patsy see **Patricia**

Paul derives from Latin and means 'small'. In spite of being the name adopted by St Paul in the New Testament, it failed to catch the imagination of parents before the current century. It has been one of the top fashion names of the past 20 years, given a boost by the fame of singer Paul McCartney and actor Paul Newman.

Paula see **Pauline**

Pauline is the most often used feminine form of Paul (see above) in English-speaking countries, though it has never been used as often as its popular male equivalent. Variations are Paula, Paulina and Paulette.

Pearl is one of the jewel names in vogue in Victorian times and has survived to the present day. Variations include Pearla and Pearle.

Peggy is one of the many pet forms of Margaret which has come to be thought of as an independent name. The actress Dame Peggy Ashcroft has kept the name in the public eye.

Penelope probably comes from the Greek meaning 'a bobbin' or 'weaver'. It has been used as a Christian name in Britain since the 1500s. In Ireland the name has been equated with Fenella. The usual abbreviations are Pen and Penny. A well-known bearer is actress Penelope Keith.

Penny see **Penelope**

Percy comes from the name of a place in Normandy. The famous

Northumbrian family of that name were associates of William the Conqueror. The name was generally used until the end of the 19th century but seems now to have faded out.

Perry began as the short form of Peregrine, from the Latin for 'a traveller' but has been a name in its own right for over a century. It has been used frequently in recent years, helped along by the popularity of the singer Perry Como.

Peter stems from the Greek word meaning 'a rock'. It was the name given to his disciple Simon by Jesus. It was out of favour after the Reformation but it came back into fashion this century. Well-known bearers include the actors Peter O'Toole and the late Peter Sellers. The shortened name is Pete.

Petula comes from the Latin 'seeker', but with Petra is sometimes looked on as a feminine form of Peter. Singer Petula Clark is the best known bearer of the name.

Philip is from the Greek meaning 'fond of horses' and was the name of one of the apostles. It was popular in the Middle Ages and in the 1900s has been back in favour again, partly because of Prince Philip, Duke of Edinburgh. The alternative spelling is Phillip and short forms are Phil and Pip.

Philippa and the modern short form Pippa are the feminine versions of Philip (see above). Both forms have been at their most popular in the past decade.

Philomena is an unusual girl's name that derives from the Greek for 'nightingale', sometimes given as 'lover of the moon'. Phil is the short form.

Phoebe means 'the shining one' and was one of the names given by the ancient Greeks to the moon goddess. It caught the imagination of Victorian parents and is still used today.

Phyllis means 'leafy', coming from the name of a maiden in Greek mythology who turned into a tree after she had killed herself for love. The pet name is Phil.

Piers is an early French version of Peter (see page 99), meaning 'rock', which came to England with the Normans. It is still used frequently by parents. Another version of the name is Pearce or Pierce.

Pippa see **Phillipa**

Polly is an old affectionate form of Mary, which is believed to have come about as a rhyming version of Molly.

Poppy comes from Latin word for 'red flower'.

Portia is a Latin name and means 'an offering to God'. It was made popular by Shakespeare's *Merchant of Venice*.

Primrose is one of the flower names introduced in the late 19th century.

Priscilla comes from the Latin word for 'ancient'. It was in vogue with the 18th century Puritans and again with the Victorians. A modern short form is Cilla which was popularized by singer Cilla Black.

Prudence was one of the most popular virtue names introduced in the 17th century and still going strong. Prue or Pru is the short form, as in Prue Leith, restaurateur and food writer.

Prunella means 'little plum' in Latin, or 'plum-coloured' in French. The date of its first use is unknown. In the present day actress Prunella Scales has publicized the name.

Quentin is from the Latin meaning 'fifth' and was in early times used for the fifth son. Sir Walter Scott's novel *Quentin Durward* publicized the name in the 19th century. Another spelling is Quintin but both names are uncommon.

Rachel means 'ewe' in Hebrew. It appears in the Old Testament and has always been a favourite with Jewish families, but in the past decade it has become generally very fashionable. Other versions are Rachael and Rachelle and it is abbreviated to Rae or Ray.

Ralph comes from the Anglo-Saxon word meaning 'wolf-counsel' and is a name which has survived from ancient times, prounced Rafe until quite recently. It made its biggest impact earlier this century. The pet form is Ralphie.

Ramona is the feminine form of Ramon, the Spanish version of Raymond (see below).

Rana is of Asian origin and means 'a queen of birth'.

Randal is a very old name derived from two Anglo-Saxon words meaning 'shield' and 'wolf'. In the Middle Ages it gave rise to surnames like Randal, Randle and Ranson. By the 18th century Randolph had appeared as a variation. The American short form Randy is seldom used in Britain.

Raoul is the French form of the old version of Ralph, and is occasionally used in English-speaking countries.

Raphaela is from Hebrew and means 'healed by God'.

Raymond derives from two Old German words meaning 'counsel' and 'protection' and came to England with the Normans. Parents used it sparingly this century when it came into vogue in most English-speaking countries. Another spelling is Raymund and the usual abbreviation is Ray, often used as an independent name.

Rebecca is a Hebrew name of uncertain origin, possibly meaning 'a knotted cord' and, in the Bible, Rebecca was Isaac's wife. The Puritans liked the name and it has come back as a favourite in recent years. Rebekah, the original Biblical spelling, is a frequent variation, the pet form being Becky.

Regina comes from the Latin for 'queen'. Reine or Raine is a variant from the French. Queenie is sometimes used as an alternative, and Rena and Gina are short forms.

Reginald comes from two Old English words meaning 'power' and 'force' and in early times the name appeared as Reynold. Its use faded out, to revive in the 19th century. Short forms are Reg, Reggie and Rex (see below).

Reid or Reed comes from the Old English word for red. It is a surname which has come to be used as a first name, particularly in the USA.

Renée is a French name derived from the Latin and meaning 'born again', which also gives the names Renata and Renate. It has never been very fashionable but is used more often than the masculine version René. Renny is an alternative spelling.

Reuben means 'behold a son' in Hebrew and, in the Old Testament, was the name of one of Jacob's sons. It has been used in Britain for 300 years, mainly, though not exclusively, by Jewish parents.

Rex is from the Latin for 'king' and has been used for about 100 years. It is also the pet form of Reginald (see above).

Rhoda derives from Greek and means 'rose' and though it appears in the New Testament it has only been in general use since the 17th century. Variations are Rhodah and Roda.

Rhona is of uncertain origin; it may stem from a contraction of Rowena (see page 105) or a Scottish place name. It first appeared about 100 years ago and has been used on the whole by Scottish parents.

Rhonda is a place name in Wales that has also been used as a girl's name, particularly in the USA.

Rhys means 'rash' or 'impetuous' and has always been a favourite Welsh name which has produced surnames like Rees and Rice.

Richard comes from Old German meaning 'stern ruler'. It was one of the names brought to England by the Normans and has been popular ever since. Well-known name-bearers include actors Richard Burton, Richard Attenborough and Richard Briers. Pet forms are Dick, Dickie, Rich, Rick, Ricky and Ritchie.

Rick and **Ricky** see **Derek**, **Eric** and **Richard**

Rita is a diminutive of Margarita, the German form of Margaret (see page 85), meaning 'pearl'. It has been used as an independent name since the turn of the century and was given a boost in popularity by the fame of actress Rita Hayworth. A contemporary bearer of the name is actress Rita Tushingham.

Robert is derived from two Old English words meaning 'fame' and 'bright' and has been a favourite with parents for 900 years. Its many pet names include Bob, Bobby, Rob and, in Scotland, Rab and Rabbie. Among the famous Roberts are poet Robert Burns and actors Robert Mitchum and Robert Redford. Roberta is the feminine version.

Robin was originally another version of Rob, the diminutive of Robert (see above) but has been established as an independent name for several hundred years, sometimes rivalling Robert in popularity. Broadcaster Sir Robin Day keeps the name before the public. The first feminine form was Robina but Robin or Robyn is now used for girls as well as boys.

Roderick derives from two Old German words meaning 'fame' and 'rule' and has always been more popular with Scottish than English parents. It is often spelt Roderic and shortened to Rod and Roddy.

Rodney evolved from a place name meaning 'reed island' which became a surname before parents began using it at christenings in honour of the famous 18th century Lord Rodney. It is usually abbreviated to Rod or Roddy (for example, actors Rod Steiger and Roddy McDowall)

Roger is from two Anglo-Saxon words meaning 'fame' and 'spear'. It was a common name in the Middle Ages but went out of use for a long period before coming back into favour this century. It has been publicized in recent years by actor Roger Moore who achieved stardom playing the James Bond character.

Roland comes from two Old German words meaning 'fame' and 'land' and came to England with the Normans. The older spelling is Rowland but the French version Roland is now more popular. The usual diminutive is Roly.

Rona may be a short form of Rowena, an alternative spelling of Rhona, a feminine version of Ronald or taken from the Gaelic word for a seal. It occurs most often in Scotland.

Ronald stems from an Old Norse name and began as the Scottish equivalent of Reginald (see page 102), meaning 'power' and 'force'. During the presidency of Ronald Reagan, Americans used it more often than British parents. Ron and Ronnie are the short forms. Comedians Ronnie Barker and Ronnie Corbett have kept the name in the public eye in recent years.

Rory is from the Gaelic for 'red' or 'ruddy'. Three kings of Ireland bore the name which has spread beyond Ireland and Scotland in recent years. Ruari is the old spelling.

Rosalie derives from a Latin word meaning 'rose'. The older version is Rosalia but the French form Rosalie has been more successful with modern parents.

Rosalind meant 'horse-serpent' in Old German and 'pretty rose' in Spanish, so there has been much dispute about its origins. Shakespeare made it popular by using it for the heroine of his play, *As You Like It* and it has survived the centuries. Alternative spellings include Rosaline, Rosalyn and Roslyn and the abbreviated form is Ros.

Rosamund comes originally from Old German meaning 'horse-protection' but in the Middle Ages scholars decided that it was from Latin, with the more attractive meaning 'rose of the world'. A modern spelling is Rosamond.

Rose and Rosa came into use because of their Old German meaning 'horse', an animal much admired, but it is because of the association with the flower that the name has endured, with a number of variations. Princess Margaret's second name is Rose.

Rosemary means 'dew of the sea', from Latin, and was introduced as one of the plant names fashionable as given names in late Victorian times. It became steadily more popular in the first half of this century, sometimes used in the French form Rosemarie.

Roslyn is a Scottish place name used as a girl's name. Some of its variations, such as Rosalyn, suggest it is closely associated with Rosalind.

Ross was originally a Celtic place name meaning 'promontory', taken first as a surname and then used as a first name in most English-speaking countries in recent years.

Rowan is becoming increasingly popular as a name for girls or boys. It comes from the rowan tree, which was believed to have the power to drive away evil. A well-known bearer is the comedian Rowan Atkinson.

Rowena is probably derived from a Celtic word for 'slender' though it may be from Old English meaning 'famous friend'. Parents took it up as a forename after Sir Walter Scott called the heroine of *Ivanhoe* Rowena in 1819 and it has been used steadily ever since.

Roxana comes from the Persian word for 'dawn' and was the heroine of a novel of that name by Daniel Defoe. Roxane is an alternative spelling and Roxy the short form.

Roy is from the Gaelic for 'red'. Though originally an extremely popular Scottish name it was very successful all over Britain, as well as other English-speaking countries, early this century when many short names were in vogue. Well-known British name-bearers are the politician Roy Jenkins and entertainers Roy Castle and Roy Hudd.

Royston is a surname taken from a place name in Yorkshire and used occasionally as a personal name since the 18th century.

Ruby is a Gem name, however it has not been widely used in recent years.

Rufus comes from the Latin for red-haired and was originally used by Jewish families as an alternative to Reuben. It is now in common use particularly in the United States.

Rupert was originally a German name from the same root as Robert (see page 103), meaning 'fame-bright'. It came to England in the 17th century through the fame of Rupert of the Rhine and though it has never been popular, it has lasted through the generations. Actor Rupert Everett and newspaper proprietor Rupert Murdoch are two of the modern Ruperts.

Russell comes from a surname which, in turn, derives from a French nickname for 'redhead'. It has been fairly popular with British parents in recent years and is publicized by astrologer Russell Grant. Another spelling is Russel and pet names are Russ and Rusty.

Ruth, probably from the Hebrew meaning 'friend', was one of the heroines of the Old Testament and became one of the Biblical names fashionable in the 17th century. Parents have been using it regularly ever since. Its usual diminutive or affectionate form is Ruthie.

Ryan is a modern first name taken from an Irish surname of unknown meaning. It has become very popular with both British and American parents, helped along by the fame of actor Ryan O'Neal.

Sabina stems from the Latin meaning 'from the Sabine region'. It has been used as a personal name in Britain for 300 years though it has never been fashionable. Alternative spellings are Sabin and Sabine.

Sabrina comes from a poetic Roman name for the river Severn, though the original meaning is not known. In recent years it has been used more often in America than Britain and can be shortened to Brina or Brie.

Sacha is from Greek, meaning 'helper of mankind'. It is used both as a boy's and a girl's name.

Sally was originally used as a pet name for Sarah (see page 108), meaning 'princess', but has been established as a name in its own right for 200 years, with its own diminutive of Sal and the alternative spelling Sallie. Actress Sally Field is a popular contemporary bearer of the name.

Samantha is of obscure origins but has been one of the great successes of the 20th century, becoming a favourite all over the English-speaking world. It has had a great boost from its use in a popular American TV series called *Bewitched*. Sam and Sammy are the short forms. Actress Samantha Eggar also popularized the name.

Samuel means 'name of God' in Hebrew and, because of its Biblical associations, was popular with the Puritans after the Reformation. It has been used steadily ever since and the usual short forms are Sam and Sammy. Sam Goldwyn, founder of MGM in Hollywood, was a well-known bearer of the name.

Sandra is a fairly modern name which began as a diminutive of the Italian name Alessandra, itself a version of Alexandra (see page 18), so the original meaning was 'defender of men'. It reached its height of popularity in the 1960s when Sandie Shaw was a favourite singer. An alternative form is Zandra and pet names are Sandy and Sandie.

Sandy see **Alexander** and **Sandra**

Sarah stems from Hebrew meaning 'princess' and was the name of Abraham's wife in the Old Testament. It was very popular for 300 years until it went out of vogue at the turn of the century, only to make a great comeback as one of today's favourites. Another spelling is Sara and the usual abbreviations are Sally and Sadie.

Saul means 'asked for' in Hebrew and appears in the Bible as the first king of Israel and Saul of Tarsus, who became St Paul. It has been used as a forename in Britain since the 17th century.

Scarlett is originally a Middle English word meaning 'colour of scarlet'. However it came immediately to the fore because of the heroine of the novel, *Gone With the Wind* – Scarlett O'Hara.

Scott comes from a surname meaning 'a Scotsman' and has only been used as a personal name this century, becoming very successful in both Scotland, England and the USA over the past 20 years, perhaps helped by the revival of interest in Scott Joplin's particular kind of music.

Sean is the Irish form of John (see page 72), meaning 'God is gracious' which evolved from the Norman French name Jean. It has been well used over the past generation, given a boost in popularity by actor Sean Connery. Other versions are Shaun and the American Shane and a feminine form is Shaune.

Sebastian derives from Greek meaning 'majestic' and was made famous by the martyred 3rd century saint. It was a popular medieval name which later fell out of favour and only revived this century. Olympic athlete Sebastian Coe helps to keep it in the public eye. Its shortened form is Seb.

Selwyn comes from the Anglo-Saxon for 'house-friend' and began as a surname. In the 19th century Welsh parents took it up as a first name. It was publicized by politician Selwyn Lloyd and has been used more widely this century.

Shane see **Sean**

Shannon comes from Gaelic and means 'old wise one'. It can be used for either a boy or a girl.

Sharon means 'the plain' in Hebrew and appears as a place name in the Bible. When first used, in the 17th century, it was a boy's name but when it came into fashion in the middle of the present century it was used only for girls. Variations include Sharron, Sharan and Sharene and diminutives are Shari and Shara.

Sheena is the English pronounciation of the name Sine, which is the Gaelic for Jane (see page 69) and its use has been spreading in recent years. Variations are Sheenagh, Sheena and Sheona.

Sheila comes from the English pronounciation of the Irish name Sile, a form of Celia (see page 32) meaning 'heavenly'. Its Irish origins were forgotten when it became popular all over Britain in the first half of the present century.

Sheldon is an Anglo-Saxon name meaning 'from the hill ledge'. It is a surname that has begun to be used as a first name.

Shelley stems from an Old English place name meaning 'clearing on a slope' which became first a surname then a personal name for boys. This century it has become well known in the English-speaking world as a girl's name, helped by actress Shelley Winters.

Sheree is the English version of the French word *chérie* meaning 'darling'. American parents prefer the Sherry spelling and other variations are Sheri and Sherri.

Sheridan evolved as a surname which was used as a boy's first name for more than 100 years, with parents showing more interest since writer Sheridan Morley publicized it.

Shirley is taken from a surname which developed from the common English place name meaning 'shire meadow'. Novelist Charlotte Brontë first used it as a girl's name for her heroine in *Shirley* in 1849 and it has been very successful this century. Well-known bearers include the actresses Shirley Temple and Shirley Maclaine and the politician Shirley Williams.

Sidney is believed to be a contraction of the French 'St Denis' and is the surname of the famous English family to which Sir Philip Sidney belonged. In Ireland Sidney has long been used as a girl's name. Sydney is an alternative spelling.

Simon stems from the Greek name meaning 'snub-nosed' and was made famous as the name of the apostle Simon Peter. It was common in the Middle Ages but completely out of favour after the Reformation. It revived to become very popular this century. Actors Simon Ward and Simon Macorkindale are modern bearers of this name. Simone is the feminine version, more popular in France than in England.

Siobhan is the Irish form of Joan (see page 71), meaning 'grace of God', and is a favourite girl's name in Ireland and to a lesser extent, Scotland. Publicized by actress Siobhan McKenna, its English variations include Shavon and Shevon.

Solomon is a Hebrew name meaning 'little man of peace'. Sol and Solly are the usual short forms. Politician Sir Solly Zuckerman was a famous 20th century bearer of the name.

Sonia was originally a Russian pet form of Sophia (see 'Sophie' below), adopted by English-speaking parents to become popular this century, with the spelling variations of Sonya and Sonja.

Sophie is the modern French form of Sophia, from the Greek meaning 'wisdom'. Sophia was a favourite name with European royal families, its use in Britain dating back to the 17th century. Sophie is a modern variation, now found more frequently than Sophia.

Soroya is a Persian name meaning 'seven stars'.

Spencer began as an old French surname meaning 'dispenser of supplies' and has been used as a given name for nearly 200 years, becoming more popular in the present generation. Actor Spencer Tracy helped to publicize the name, which sometimes appears as Spenser.

Stacey probably started life as a pet form of Eustacia or Anastasia but has become popular as an independent name in its own right with modern parents and a top favourite in the USA. Variations are Stacy, Stacie and Stacia.

Stanley comes from a surname derived from a common English name meaning 'stony field'. It has been used as a first name for about 200 years and only became popular in the late 19th century, after the explorer Henry Stanley's famous meeting with Dr Livingstone. It made its greatest impact in the early years of this century and famous Stanleys include Prime Minister Stanley Baldwin and footballer Stanley Matthews. The usual abbreviation is Stan.

Stella is the Latin for 'star'. The name was almost unknown before the 16th century poet Sir Philip Sidney made it famous in his sonnets and parents only began using it in large numbers at the beginning of this century. Variations are Estella and Estelle, which has been used more often in recent years.

Stephanie is the feminine form of the French version of Stephen (see below). It appeared for the first time early this century and has been very successful in the past two decades. Stefanie is a modern alternative spelling. Princess Stephanie of Monaco is a modern bearer of the name.

Stephen comes from the Greek for 'garland' or 'crown' and was the name of several saints, including the first Christian martyr. It was common in the Middle Ages leading to surnames such as Stephens, Stevenson and Stimpson. Though it became neglected in the late 1800s, it made a comeback as one of the top favourites in the middle of this century. Steven is a frequent alternative spelling and short forms are Steve and Stevie. Well-known bearers include the late actor Steve McQueen and snooker champion Steve Davis.

Stuart comes from the Old English for 'steward' and was a surname made famous by Stuart kings and queens. It came into use as a first name either as Stuart or Stewart, in the 19th century and has been very popular over the past decade. Diminutives are Stu, Stewie and Stew.

Susan derives from the Hebrew for 'lily' and in the older form, Susannah, is a Biblical name used in Britain since the 13th century. In modern times Susan took over to become one of the most widely used girls' names in the English-speaking world. French forms are Suzanne and Suzette. Short forms include the old-fashioned Suky as well as Sue and Susie. Famous Susans include the actresses Susan Hayward and Susan Hampshire.

Sybil comes from the name given to women who interpreted the oracles in ancient Greece and the Normans brought it to Britain. The early spelling was Sibyl but Sybil has taken over since the 19th century, with variations such as Sybilla and Sybel. Abbreviations are Syb and Sybbie.

Sylvia derives from the Latin word for 'wood'. In the 17th and 19th centuries the name was used mainly by poets, then parents took it up and made it popular in the first half of this century. Silvia is the alternative spelling and the diminutive form is Sylvie.

Tabitha is Hebrew and means 'gazelle'. It became popular in recent times due to the success of the TV series *Bewitched*.

Tamara is from Hebrew and means 'palm tree'. It has been growing in popularity in recent times.

Tammy see **Tamsin**

Tamsin was originally a pet form of the name Thomasina, the feminine form of Thomas (see page 114), meaning 'twin'. When Thomasina disappeared, Tamsin survived in Cornwall and it caught the imagination of parents again this century. The short form Tammy is used a a name in its own right. Author and journalist Tamsin Day Lewis is a contemporary bearer of the name.

Tania or Tanya, is a shortening of the name Tatiana, though its meaning is unknown. It has been frequently used in Britain as an independent name over the past 20 years.

Tara comes from an Irish place name meaning 'crag' which began as a given name in the USA and came to Britain quite recently, quickly becoming fashionable.

Ted see **Edward**

Terence derives from a Roman clan name but its meaning is unknown. British parents started using it about 100 years ago and by the middle of this century it was very popular. The abbreviation Terry is sometimes used as an independent name. Well-known bearers are the British actor Terence Stamp and the designer and businessman Sir Terence Conran.

Teresa is of unknown origin but may stem from the Greek word meaning 'reaper'. It began as a Spanish name, spreading among Roman Catholica families all over the world with the fame of St Teresa of Avila in the 16th century. More recently it has been successful as Terese and Theresa and the modern pet forms are Terry and Terri.

Terry see **Terence** and **Teresa**

Tessa and Tess began as Old English pet names for Teresa but have long been used as names in their own right, with their own diminutive Tessie.

Thelma is a name invented by the Victorian novelist Marie Corelli which is still in regular use.

Theodore derives from the Greek meaning 'God's gift'. The name only came into general use in Britain in the 19th century. It has always been more popular in the USA than Britain and was given a boost by the popularity of President Theodore Roosevelt. An alternative spelling is Theodor. The Welsh version is Tudor and the Russian one is Fyodor. Theo is the usual British pet form but in the USA Ted and Teddy are used.

Thomas means 'twin' in Hebrew and was the name of one of the disciples in the New Testament. It caught the public imagination following the murder of Thomas à Becket in the 12th century and has been one of the best known boys' names ever since. Abbreviations are Tom, Tommy and Thom and today Tom is often used as a name in its own right. Famous bearers include the novelist Thomas Hardy and the actor Tom Courtenay.

Tiffany was originally the short form of the vanished name Theophania, from the Greek 'manifestation of God', given to girls born at Epiphany. Tiffany has undergone a revival recently.

Tilly see **Matilda**

Timothy means 'honouring of God' in Greek and was the name of St Paul's companion in the New Testament. It was used along with other Biblical names after the Reformation and has been fashionable among British parents in recent years. The usual abbreviations are Tim and Timmy.

Tina started life as a pet form for any name ending in 'ina', such as Clementina or Bettina and has survived many of them to become and independent and popular name.

Toby is the English version of Tobias, from the Hebrew meaning 'the Lord is good', now used by young parents as an independent name.

Todd comes from the surname meaning 'fox', taken up by parents as a given name in recent years, though it is used less often in Britain than in the USA. Another spelling is Tod.

Tom see **Thomas**

Toni is an abbreviated form of Antonia, and is used as a girl's name in its own right. The spelling distinguishes it from the boy's name Tony.

Tonia is a short form of Antoinette which is now recognized as an individual name.

Tracey is a modern name which may have evolved from a version of Teresa (see page 114) or from a Norman surname. Over the past 20 years it has been a favourite with British and American parents, though its greatest popularity peak has now passed.

Travis and Travers may come from the French for 'crossroads' or from the English surname and are unusual names in Britain. They are far more frequently used in other English-speaking countries, especially Australia.

Trent is a place name which is strictly speaking a surname, but which has been used as a boy's name in recent years.

Trevor evolved from a Welsh place name meaning 'great homestead', and was first used as a personal name in the 1800s. It was in vogue around the middle of this century, the Welsh form being Trefor and the usual abbreviation is Trev.

Tristram comes from the Celtic for 'tumult' and the form Tristan is linked with the French word for 'sad'. Tristram has survived since the 12th century as a name for boys, though it has never been popular and Tristan, famous from the legend of Tristan and Isolde, is just as likely to be used today.

Trixie see **Beatrice**

Troy probably comes from a French place name which turned into a surname and was later used as a personal name in the USA. British parents were quite slow to take it up but have used it quite often over the past 20 years.

Trudy began life as a pet form of Gertrude and Ermintrude, both names which have faded out of modern use and is now a well-established independent name with the alternative spellings Trudi and Trudie.

Tyrone developed from the Irish place name meaning 'Owen's country' and was publicized by actor Tyrone Power. American parents took it up, then it caught the imagination of British parents and was used quite often in the 1960s.

Una is the English spelling of the ancient Irish name Oonagh and its meaning is uncertain; it may be linked with the Latin for 'one' or the Irish for 'lamb'. It has been used outside Ireland for over a century and actress Una Stubbs has publicized the name in recent years. The original spelling Oonagh is still used.

Unity is a virtue name introduced by the Puritans in the 17th century. Unity Mitford is a famous bearer of the name.

Ursula derives from the Latin for 'she-bear' and was made famous by the 5th century saint, martyred along with 11,000 virgins. It was popular in medieval times, then again in the 17th century and has survived the generations, though it is no longer a favourite. Variations are Ursa, Ursel and Ursella and it is shortened to Ursie. The actress Ursula Andress has helped to spread the name.

Valentine is derived from the Latin meaning 'healthy' and 'strong'. The St Valentine whose feast day is celebrated by lovers was a 3rd century martyr. It is still sometimes used as a boy's name, though formerly was used for girls as well.

Valerie originated in the feminine form of a famous Roman family name, probably meaning 'to be in good health'. It was used in Victorian times as Valeria but Valerie, coming to England from France, soon took over. It was very successful in the first half of this century and is still used regularly. Another spelling is Valery and the usual abbreviation is Val.

Van is from the Dutch meaning 'of' or 'from'. It has become popular as a name in its own right whereas it used to simply be a surname prefix.

Vanessa was invented by the 18th century writer Jonathan Swift as the name of one of his characters, based partly on the name Esther (see page 49). Parents were slow to take it up as a personal name but it has been used quite often since the middle of this century, boosted by the fame of the actress Vanessa Redgrave. Pet names are Ness, Nessie and Vanni.

Vaughan was originally a Welsh surname meaning 'little' and has been used as a first name since the end of the 19th century. Usually a boys' name, it is occasionally used for girls. An alternative spelling is Vaughn.

Velma see **Wilhemina**

Vera is from the Russian word for 'faith' and came into use in late Victorian times, when Russian names were in vogue. It made its greatest impact in the first half of this century, and well-known bearers of the name are the writer Vera Brittain and the singer Vera Lynn.

Verity, comes from the Latin for 'truth', was one of the many virtue names given to girls by the 17th century Puritans. It has remained in use ever since but has never been common. Another spelling is Verita. Businesswoman Verity Lambert is a modern bearer of the name.

Vernon comes from a common French place name meaning 'alder tree' which came to Britain as a Norman surname. It was adopted as a personal name in the 19th century and did well in the early 1900s. The short form is Vern.

Veronica derives from the Latin for 'true image' and was the name given to the woman who wiped the face of Jesus with a cloth which retained the image of his face. As Véronique it was a popular name in France long before it reached Scotland in the 17th century, only spreading to England during the past 100 years. It is abbreviated to Nicky and Ronnie.

Victor means 'conqueror' in Latin and was the name of an early pope and several Christian martyrs. It has been used in England since the 13th century and became popular because of its similarity to Victoria. It is often shortened to Vic or Vick.

Victoria is the Latin word for 'victory' and was hardly ever used as a given name in Britain before Queen Victoria came to the throne. Even then it was normally used a second name and only became a favourite in recent years. Other versions are Victorie and Victorine and the many pet forms include Vicky, Vicki and Vikki. A well-known modern bearer is the actress Victoria Principal.

Vincent stems from the Latin meaning 'conquering' and was made famous by St Vincent of Saragossa, a 3rd-century martyr. It was used in medieval England but went through a spell in the doldrums before being revived in the 19th century. Since then it has been used consistently, never a top favourite but unaffected by fashions. It is shortened to Vince.

Viola see **Violet**

Violet is a flower name symbolizing modesty. Viola, the older Latin form as used by Shakespeare in *Twelfth Night*, gave way to the English Violet in the 19th century when the fashion for flower names was at its height.

Virginia originates from an ancient Roman clan name, probably meaning 'manly race' and has been used as a first name in England for nearly 200 years. In the USA it has different origins: parents took the name from the state of Virginia, which in turn was named after Queen Elizabeth I, the Virgin Queen. The actress Virginia McKenna and tennis champion Virginia Wade have kept the name current in recent years. Nicknames include Ginny and Jinny.

Vivian and Vivien derive from the Latin word meaning 'alive'. Vivian, the usual spelling for a boy's name, dates from medieval times but is seldom used today. The feminine form Vivien has been successful this century, making its biggest impact, with the alternative spelling Vivienne, in the 1950s.

Wade began life as an Anglo-Saxon place name meaning 'ford', which became a surname. This century it was adopted by American parents as a given name and is now used in Britain too.

Wallace is a name for boys and girls derived from an Anglo-Saxon word meaning 'foreign'. Used as a surname in Scotland, it was first used as a first name in the 19th century, but has never become widespread. Wallis is an alternative spelling sometimes used for girls. It was the first name of the late Duchess of Windsor.

Wallis see **Wallace**

Walter is from two Old German words meaning 'rule' and 'folk'. It came to England with the Norman Conquest and was common enough to give rise to surnames like Walters, Watson and Waters. Short forms are Wal and Wally and, in America, Walt. Well-known Walters include the actor Walter Matthau and Walt Disney.

Wanda has Germanic roots but its meaning is uncertain; some suggestions are 'kindred' and 'stock'.

Ward derives from the surname meaning 'guardian' or 'watchman'. Though it was used as a first name in the 19th century, it disappeared from Britain for a time, coming back in recent years.

Warren comes from the Old German meaning 'defender'. The Normans brought it to England where it became a surname but fell out of use as a first name for several hundred years. In the 19th century parents took it up again and it has been used quite often in recent years, boosted by the fame of the actor Warren Beatty.

120

Wayne is a surname meaning 'waggoner', from Old English, used as a given name in recent years, first in the USA and later in Britain.

Wendy is a name invented by playwright J.M. Barrie for the heroine of *Peter Pan* in 1904. Parents took it up a few years later and it has become a favourite. Other forms are Wenda and Wendie.

Wesley comes from an Anglo-Saxon place name meaning 'west meadow' which turned into a surname. Parents began to use it in honour of John Wesley, the 18th-century founder of the Methodists.

Wilbur is believed to be from Old German. 'Wil' meaning 'will' and 'bur' meaning defence.

Wilfred comes from two Old English words meaning 'will' and 'peace'.

Wilhemina is the feminine form of the German version of William and is especially liked in Scotland. There are numerous short forms including Willa, Velma, Mina and Minna.

William derives from two Old German words meaning 'resolution' and 'helmet' and became famous in Britain through William the Conqueror. Many surnames came from it, including Williams, Wilkes and Willis, and through the centuries it has been a top favourite. It seemed to be on the decline in the 1970s but since the birth of Prince William in 1982 it looks like coming back into fashion. Pet names are Bill, Billy, Will, Willie and Wills.

Winifred is a Welsh name meaning 'blessed reconciliation'. Short forms are Freda, Wyn or Winnie.

Winston comes from a place name originally meaning 'Wine's farm'. It is most strongly associated with the wartime leader Sir Winston Churchill. It has never been in widespread use but is favoured by families of West Indian origin.

Wyndham began life as an Anglo-Saxon place name meaning 'windy settlement', taken as a family name and, in the 1800s, as a first name. A well-known bearer was the author Wyndham Lewis.

Xavier comes from the Arabic for 'bright' and was the surname of the 16th century Spanish St Francis Xavier.

Xenia is a girl's name taken from the Greek for 'guest'. Zenia is an alternative spelling which indicates the pronunciation.

Yehudi is a Hebrew name meaning 'praise' made famous by the violinist Yehudi Menuhin but seldom used.

Yolanda is a medieval French name which is a variation on the diminutive form of Viola. Iolanthe is an alternative rendering.

Yvonne and Yvette are both feminine diminutives of the French boys' names Yves, meaning 'yew'. Yvonne has spread through the English-speaking world in modern times, though Yvette has not been nearly as successful.

Zachary is the shortened form of Zacharias, meaning 'God remembered' in Hebrew. Zacharias has almost disappeared but Zachary and its pet name Zak are both used as names in their own right.

Zara comes from an Arabic word for 'splendour of the east' and is a modern addition to the stock of English first names. It received a boost when The Princess Royal used it at her daughter's christening in 1981. Another spelling is Zaira.

Zelda is the last part of the name Grizelda.

Zita is believed to be simply the end part of the Spanish name 'Rosita'. This abbreviated form has now become popular.

Zoe is Greek for 'life'. British parents took it up in the 19th century and it is now quite fashionable.

HOROSCOPES

ARIES
21 March – 20 April

Birth Stones: *Amethyst and Diamond*
Lucky Flowers: *Daffodil and Tulip*
Famous Arians: *Elton John, Claire Francis and David Steel*

Arians, born under the sign of the Ram, learn quickly and love a challenge. Boisterous, friendly and extrovert they are outdoor types who are good at sports of all kinds. When children, Arians are constantly inquisitive and continually asking how things work. In later life they often grow up to be very practical and expert in construction and DIY.

Career sucess is very important to Arians – they want to get to the top no matter what. Blessed with boundless energy they will excel in anything that requires innovation and endless activity.

Occasionally lacking in understanding Arians are not ideal for team work – they prefer to act on their own or as leaders of a group.

TAURUS
21 April – 21 May

Birth Stones: *Emerald and Coral*
Lucky Flowers: *Violet and Poppy*
Famous Taureans: *Queen Elizabeth II, Karl Marx and Barbra Streisand*

Children born under the sign of the bull are 'slow but sure'. They seldom learn quickly but they learn well and their determination makes them sure to suceed. Their 'bullishness' can occasionally lead to stubborness and temper tantrums, though these are rare.

Taureans are excellent homemakers – they delight in their creature comforts, good food, wine and luxuries of every kind. Generous by nature and romantic, Taureans make wonderful companions, however they are prone to strong fits of jealousy.

From time to time Taureans will show a talent for coming up with brilliant imaginative ideas and this together with their famed stubborness makes them a force to be reckoned with.

GEMINI
22 May – 21 June

Birth Stones: *Topaz and Crystal*
Lucky Flowers: *Lilly of the Valley*
Famous Gemineans: *Paul McCartney, Prince Philip and Marilyn Monroe*

Gemini is the sign of the twins. Gemini people have active minds in active bodies. They are delightful because they are unpredictable and never boring – however they do have a tendency to be inconsistent and they may lack staying power.

Gemineans are born with silvery tongues and can charm the birds from the trees; they have an uncanny way of influencing others and will fascinate anybody they wish. As children they will learn to talk early and are always alert and inquisitive. They will constantly need new diversions as they are quick learners and will soon get bored.

Those born under this sign are also great communicators – they have a natural ability to convey complex ideas in a simple way. Gemineans are very caring and demonstrative in their feelings though they do have a tendency to be fickle in their emotions.

CANCER
22 June – 23 July

Birth Stones: *Pearl and Moonstone*
Lucky Flowers: *Iris and Anemone*
Famous Cancerians: *The Princess of Wales, Esther Rantzen and Lord Byron*

Cancerians, those born under the sign of the crab, are sympathetic, affectionate and loyal. They can on first meeting tend to appear rather hard, uncaring and perhaps even rough. However beneath the hard shell they are gentle and caring.

Homelife is very important to Cancerians – when they become adults their entire lives centre around their partners, children and parents. Totally reliable and steadfast they will make faithful friends, however they can be so devoted that they are easily hurt if they do not receive loyalty in equal amounts.

Cancerians have vivid imaginations and normally excel in careers where their creative talents can be used to the full.

LEO
24 July – 23 August

Birth Stones: *Ruby and Diamond*
Lucky Flowers: *Peony and Sunflower*
Famous Leos: *Dustin Hoffman, Mick Jagger and the Princess Royal*

Leo children born under the sign of the lion like to be given lots of attention; they always want to be noticed and will stand out from the crowd no matter what the occasion. Leos are the great extroverts of the zodiac – they are outgoing, sociable and constantly determined to be the life and soul of the party.

Those born under this sign are natural leaders – they can inspire others to do great things – they learn quickly but occasionally overlook detail. Leos like to take command of everything they are involved in. Genuinely convinced that they are right – they tend to make their views known to all – however the uncanny thing is that they are invariably correct!

The sign of Leo is perhaps the luckiest of all the zodiac signs and those born in it will be able to turn any disaster into a triumph.

VIRGO
24 August – 23 September

Birth Stones: *Topaz and Pink Jasper*
Lucky Flowers: *Lavender*
Famous Virgoes: *Zandra Rhodes, Mother Teresa and Peter Sellers*

Those born under Virgo, sign of the Virgin, are naturally gentle, punctual and careful with money. Possessed with a great desire for order and neatness they can be extremely efficient with a tendency to be fussy and over-critical. A Virgo child will never have an untidy bedroom! Even in the workplace Virgos cannot tolerate mess or muddle and they are ruthless when it comes to reorganizing chaos of any kind. This love of order is essential to the happiness of all born under this sign, no matter their age.

Naturally reserved Virgos find it difficult to let their hair down, however when they do socialize and when they do make friends they are likely to keep them for life.

LIBRA
24 September – 23 October

Birth Stones: *Diamond and Opal*
Lucky Flowers: *Cyclamen and Lilac*
Famous Librans: *Cliff Richard, Margaret Thatcher and Brigitte Bardot*

Librans, born in the sign of the scales, are tactful, well-balanced people with a strong sense of justice and fair play. Librans are gentle, romantic creatures who have a deep love of beautiful things. They possess great charm and arouse feelings of love and affection in all those they meet.

Librans also have an inability to 'put-off' doing even the smallest chore – this trait is not due to laziness but an unfortunate inability to make decisions. However when they do decide to act Librans can be so energetic and decisive that they can surprise even those closest to them.

Librans tend to be very popular and spend most of the time surrounded by friends. Their courteous, peaceful natures and dislike of arguments make them agreeable companions.

SCORPIO
24 October – 22 November

Birth Stones: *Topaz and Malachite*
Lucky FLowers: *Azalias and Carnations*
Famous Scorpios: *Petula Clark, Prince Charles and Indira Ghandi*

Those born under Scorpio, the scorpion, have great vitality and will power. They possess very strong emotions which are particularly evident in their romantic lives.

Scorpio children will never be dull; on the contrary they are filled with energy and may sometimes be slightly difficult to discipline. Scorpios will always have a definite idea about what they want in life and because of their determination and hard work success is sure to come their way. They possess a unique inner strength which enables them to overcome seemingly insurmountable problems.

Those born under the sign of Scorpio have a keen dislike for pettiness – they think big, act big and cannot tolerate triviality.

SAGITTARIUS
23 November – 21 December

Birth Stone: *Amethyst and Topaz*
Lucky Flowers: *Pinks and Carnations*
Famous Sagittarians: *Frank Sinatra, Winston Churchill and Noel Coward*

Sagittarians, born under the sign of the archer, are witty, intelligent and careless! All Sagittarians show enormous potential when they are children but this does not always materialize in later life. This is because those born under this sign have a very happy-go-lucky, carefree attitude which can sometimes result in them wasting valuable opportunities. They possess a penetrating honesty and are so openly generous that some people find them a little difficult to deal with.

Sagittarians place an enormous amount of importance on their freedom and they are not often keen on 'settling down'. However once they do, they become devoted partners, totally free of jealousy or possessivness.

CAPRICORN
22 December – 20 January

Birth Stones: *Jet and White Onyx*
Lucky Flowers: *Hyacinth and Pansy*
Famous Capricorns: *Shirley Bassey, Susannah York and Cecil Beaton*

Those born under the sign of the goat are self-contained, with feelings that run very strongly and deeply. Normally predictable, plodding steadily along, people born under this sign can occasionally be just a little capricious – though this is always short lived.

Capricorn children grow into good students. They are hard workers but tend to keep their ambitions to themselves, being rather secretive by nature. However they will nearly always reach their desired goal and will soon command the respect and admiration of their friends and collegues.

Sometimes those born under this sign can appear a little dull but this is normally just on the outside – inside they have a kind nature and a very sharp mind.

AQUARIUS
21 January – 19 February

Birth Stones: *Sapphire and Opal*
Lucky Flowers: *Daffodil and Orchid*
Famous Aquarians: *Ronald Reagan, Prince Andrew and Germaine Greer*

Aquarians are those born under the sign of the water carrier. They are strongly independent and need a lot of freedom otherwise they can rebel against authority. Aquarians are also strongly caring people and hate injustice of any kind – however their relish for putting things right can sometimes get them into awkward situations. Those born under this sign are excellent talkers and grow into intelligent lively people always exploring new ideas and gadgets.

Although friendly and social Aquarians have a knack for keeping themselves to themselves – those close to them will always feel that they will never completely know their Aquarian friend. When it comes to romance Aquarians prefer to seek company when it suits rather than becoming involved in a steady partnership.

PISCES
20 February – 20 March

Birth Stones: *Topaz and Amethyst*
Lucky FLowers: *Tulip and Dahlia*
Famous Pisceans: *Elizabeth Taylor, Rudolf Nureyev and John Steinbeck*

Pisceans born under the sign of the fish, are charming, good natured and compassionate. They do tend to have a strong creative imagination which sometimes means that they devote too much time to day-dreaming.

Extremely kind and loving, Pisceans give their affection readily and sometimes are deeply hurt when they are rejected. Their one major fault is that they are easily led and influenced. They tend to be decent people but if a Piscean behaves in an unpleasant way then it is because he or she is being manipulated by someone else.

Pisceans are often artistic and love painting, music and dancing, though they do sometimes suffer from a lack of ambition. Pisceans hate unpleasantness of any kind and can be extremely impractical.